Underneath It All

A HISTORY OF
WOMEN'S UNDERWEAR

AMBER J. KEYSER

TWENTY-FIRST CENTURY BOOKS / MINNEAPOLIS

S

For Lacy, who puts the voom in va-va-voom

Cover photograph: Photographer Horst P. Horst took this image of a Mainbocher corset in 1939.
It is one of the most iconic photos of fashion photography.

Twenty-First Century Books
A division of Lerner Publishing Group, Inc.
241 First Avenue North
Minneapolis, MN 55401 USA

For reading levels and more information, look up this title at www.lernerbooks.com.

Main body text set in Adrianna Condensed Demibold 11/15.
Typeface provided by Chank.

Library of Congress Cataloging-in-Publication Data

Names: Keyser, Amber J., author.
Title: Underneath it all : a history of women's underwear / by Amber J. Keyser.
Description: Minneapolis : Twenty-First Century Books, [2018] | Audience: Age: 13–18. | Audience: Grade 9
    to 12. | Includes bibliographical references and index.
Identifiers: LCCN 2017008905 (print) | LCCN 2017010951 (ebook) | ISBN 9781512425314 (lb : alk.
    paper) | ISBN 9781512498837 (eb pdf)
Subjects: LCSH: Lingerie industry—History—Juvenile literature. | Women's clothing—History—Juvenile
    literature.
Classification: LCC HD9948.3.A2 K49 2018 (print) | LCC HD9948.3.A2 (ebook) | DDC 687/.2209—dc23

LC record available at https://lccn.loc.gov/2017008905

Manufactured in the United States of America
1-41285-23244-9/12/2017

Table of Contents

Beyond Frippery and Lace

From the bust-flattening *apodesme* of the ancient Greeks to the elaborate corsets of the Victorian era to Madonna's famous cone bra from the 1990s, the history of women's underwear is far more than a bit of frippery and lace. In the beginning, these clothes protected the body from rough outerwear. They also protected outerwear from sweat. But over the centuries, intimate garments took on a much more complex role in women's lives. They shaped women's bodies to fit the ideals of female beauty. They also became a focus of eroticism within intimate relationships and in art, film, and advertising. Lingerie eventually provided a way for the wearer to express individual style and personal empowerment.

EXPOSED IN PUBLIC

On a warm August day in 2015, twenty-four-year-old Jae West made her way to Piccadilly Circus, a crowded, central hub in the city of London, England. While cars and double-decker buses were rumbling past and tourists were taking pictures, feeding pigeons, and eating lunch, West peeled off her blue, flowered sundress and tied a scarf over her own eyes.

Tentative, trembling, and wearing only a black bra and matching panties, she held out a handful of pens for the strangers on every side. She propped a sign next

During the Japanese leg of her 1990 Blond Ambition World Tour, Madonna performs in a high-fashion cone bra and garters designed by Jean Paul Gaultier. Madonna's fashions, which flaunted underwear as outerwear, provoked controversy and revolutionized fashion trends.

to her. It read, "I'm standing for anyone who has struggled with an eating disorder or self-esteem issues like me. To support self-acceptance, draw a heart on my body."

To West, those first minutes felt like hours. Her heart raced. What if no one stepped forward? What if someone made fun of her? What if, instead of

Jae West undressed to her bra and panties in a crowded public space in central London in the summer of 2015. She described it as a "public act of self-acceptance" in the hopes that we can all "appreciate the bodies that [we] are given."

acceptance, she was met with scorn? Utterly vulnerable, blindfolded, and nearly naked, West waited.

And waited.

On every side, she could feel people moving and hear them whispering. Suddenly someone took a pen from her hand. She felt the tip on her bare skin, tracing the shape of a heart. Emotions swelled through her—relief, gratitude, love—and tears spilled down her cheeks.

Soon all the pens were gone. On her chest, thighs, belly, and back, people were drawing hearts.

"You're very brave," one stranger said. "It's amazing what you're doing."

A father brought his children forward and told them, "Everyone should love themselves exactly as they are."

But through high school and into her early twenties, West hadn't loved her body. She's not alone. The Centre for Appearance Research (CAR) based in Bristol, England, is the largest research group in the world focusing on the role of appearance and body image in people's lives. According to a 2012 CAR study, 60 percent of adults reported "feeling ashamed of the way they look." Standing in a public place wearing nothing but underwear is the last thing that most people would consider doing. However, West inspired others such as Amy Pence—a self-described "fat feminist mother" of three—to follow her lead. Pence says, "I've made peace with my body."

About her own experience in Piccadilly Circus, West said, "If everyone could know and appreciate how beautiful they are from childhood I think this world would be a very different place."

Being naked or nearly naked is a vulnerable state. The body is laid bare to society's expectations about physical beauty. We are exposed to judgment, both from others and from ourselves. Jae West's public act of undressing reveals the ways in which undergarments are both a private and a public layer of clothing. The history of these garments illuminates the complex interactions of gender, sexuality, politics, and body image.

CHAPTER ONE

Leather and Linen

Undergarments were once a secret. In the twenty-first century, lingerie is out in the open—on the streets, on TV, in movies, on the glossy covers of fashion magazines, on billboards, and in window displays full of satin and lace, cleavage and curves. What was once hidden has gradually been revealed. The history of women's underwear from then to now begins with . . . nothing. Unless you count fig leaves from Bible stories.

ANCIENT UNDIES

Some of the earliest information historians have about female fashion comes from ancient Egyptian art and artifacts dating back about five thousand years. In the moderate, temperate climate of the region, women wore loose linen tunics with nothing underneath.

The fashions during ancient Greek and Roman times thousands of years later were similar to ancient Egyptian clothing. Women wore long, flowing gowns but with something new—undergarments. Beneath their gowns, Greek and Roman women wore straps or bands made of cloth or leather called *apodesme* in Greek and *strophium* in Latin (the language of ancient Rome). Women tied these garments across their chests to flatten their breasts. They tied *zona*, usually made from strips of linen, to cinch the waist and hips. Versions of this garment for girls were called *fascia*.

A beautiful ancient Roman mosaic floor in Sicily, dating to about 400–300 BCE, depicts ten women wearing what look like strapless leather bras and bikini underwear. Commonly referred to as the bikini girls, they are clearly exercising. As most twenty-first-century women would agree, it would make sense to wear the leather *strophium* to bind and constrain the breasts while working out. And you have to have something on your bottom half, right?

Known as the bikini girls, these athletic women on an ancient mosaic floor sport leather garments, similar to modern-day bandeau bras and bikini bottoms. The Roman mosaic in eastern Sicily dates back to the third century BCE and once adorned a private villa.

Archaeologists excavating Roman wells in London discovered a leather string bikini like those depicted in the mosaic of the ten Roman maidens in Sicily. Yet experts find no evidence in ancient written texts that Roman women regularly wore underwear. Some historians suggest that acrobats or dancers wore the bikinis. Others think women may have worn them only during their menstrual cycle to hold absorbent rags.

"OBSCENE" GARMENTS

Before and during the Han dynasty, from 206 BCE to 220 CE, women's undergarments in ancient China were called *xieyi*. In English this word means "obscene," but it can also be used to mean something like "frivolous." Either way, underwear was definitely not out in the open in ancient China. Instead, a sense of shame and repression accompanies early descriptions of the garments, which were said to remove desire as well as to protect the heart and belly from disease.

The earliest known *xieyi* were tunics to cover the breasts and stomach. The tunics were made from a piece of fabric shaped like a small apron. Straps went over the shoulders, crossed mid-back, and were then tied to straps at the sides of the garment. In later dynasties (from 420 CE into the first decade of the twentieth century), Chinese women wore undergarments similar to *xieyi*. Some, called *moxiong,* were triangular, tying behind the neck and at the sides. Others, called *zhuyao,* were more like tube tops. Both were worn tightly bound around the chest.

During these periods in Chinese history, women's outerwear was not an opportunity for women to get creative. A woman's clothing was determined by social rank, and she had very limited style and color options to choose from. But next to her skin, a woman found her one chance at self-expression. Her delicate undergarments, especially among the upper classes, were often made of silk and were decorated with elaborate, colorful embroidery and sometimes lace, feathers, or fur. Undergarments became highly eroticized through artwork and writings known as pillow books. Much of what we surmise about women's undergarments in ancient China comes from these sources. Created by men, the works served men's sexual fantasies. They were not actually meant to record the everyday practices and fashions of women. It's unclear what regular women, especially those of the lower classes, would have worn.

One ancient Chinese undergarment persists in modern fashions. The *dudou* is known from as early as 206 BCE. It is a version of the *xieyi* and covers the chest and belly. In ancient times, it sometimes also had a pocket to

Twenty-first-century tailors in China still design and sew variations of ancient undergarments known as *xieyi* and *dudou*. They can be worn as lingerie or as outerwear.

hold ginger or other medicinal herbs. Style and design have changed through time, but by the Qing dynasty (ca. 1644–1912 CE), the *dudou* had morphed into a diamond-shaped slip of fabric tied loosely over the breasts. Contemporary designers such as Taiwanese American Irene Lu at Pillowbook include the *dudou* in upscale lingerie lines. The Pillowbook *dudou* can be worn either by itself as a halter top or as a piece of lingerie underneath other clothing.

STAYING WARM, KEEPING CLEAN

In medieval Europe (also known as the Middle Ages, 500–1500 CE), one of the primary functions of undergarments (also called body linens because they were often made of linen) was to protect the body from the cold. Dressing was all about layers, with the softest fabrics near the skin. Besides insulation, the linens protected the body from rougher outerwear. Historians believe that medieval women most likely did not wear underpants. Instead, they wore only a simple T-shaped shift (also called a smock, or a chemise). Like a nightgown, it had long sleeves and was fairly shapeless. Wealthy women and royalty wore fancier shifts made of finely woven fabric and decorated with elaborate embroidery.

The shift kept outerwear clean by absorbing sweat and other bodily fluids. Most women could afford to have multiple linen shifts, which they could change when they became soiled and were relatively easy to clean. But women's dresses, especially those made from delicate, heavy, or otherwise hard-to-launder fabrics such as silk, lace, hemp, wool, and leather, didn't get washed much, if at all. Wearing body linens protected and prolonged the life of these valuable garments.

In all but the richest households, laundry was done once or twice a year. Women or their maids sprinkled dirty linens with ashes to prevent mold until the garments could be cleaned. On wash day, women either hauled dirty clothes and homemade soap to nearby rivers or hauled water to their homes, where they worked over large cauldrons of boiling hot water. First, they dampened, soaped, and left the clothes to soak. Then they boiled the clothes in a large vat of water, scrubbed them on a washboard with more soap, and rinsed them in clean water. Sometimes they bleached linens with old urine (which contains ammonia, a natural bleach) from household chamber pots (toilets) or with lye (made from ashes and water). Oil stains could be removed with a paste made of wheat bran or chalk mixed with turpentine. If that wasn't enough to get linens clean, women did it again. When the washing was done, they stretched the clothes manually to keep their shape, dried them on clotheslines in the sun, starched them, and ironed them—all by hand. Washing an entire household's laundry could take days.

LOADING UP THE BREAST BAGS

Until recently, most historians of fashion thought that the first bras appeared in the late nineteenth century. Then, in 2008, an archaeological find in Austria upset that timeline. During renovations of Lengberg Castle, archaeologists from the University of Innsbruck found a vault filled with well-preserved leather and textiles hidden under the floorboards of a second-story room. In this tossed-away treasure trove, archaeologists found four medieval-era bras. Radiocarbon dating by historian Beatrix Nutz indicated the bras were made between 1390 and 1485 CE. Unlike the chest straps of the ancient Greeks and Romans, these linen garments had defined breast cups. One, in particular, with wide straps over the shoulders and a chest band with cups, was surprisingly modern in its design. Another one was shaped like a halter top, with cups made from two strips of fabric sewn together. It tied behind the neck, and thin strips of fabric allowed the wearer to tie the bra snugly around the chest.

This discovery illuminated some confusing references in medieval literature to items called breast bags, which contemporary scholars had long puzzled over. For example, in *Cyrurgia* (or Surgery), one of the Western's world's first medical books, French royal surgeon Henri de Mondeville (ca. 1260–1320) wrote, "Some women . . . insert two bags in their dresses, adjusted to the breasts, fitting tight, and they put them [the breasts] into them [the bags] every morning and fasten them when possible with a matching band." Before the discovery of the Lengberg bras, no one really knew what de Mondeville was talking about. The bra discovery doesn't mean that all women were loading their breast bags every morning. Since these artifacts were found in a castle, some scholars think that their use may have been restricted to the nobility.

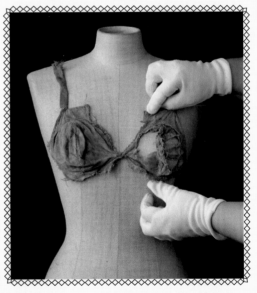

This well-preserved bra, dating back to the fifteenth century, revealed the first clue that women may have worn modern-style bras long before historians thought. Some of the bras found in Lengberg Castle included decorative lace at the bottom of the cups.

Archaeologists also found a pair of underwear in a trash heap at Lengberg Castle. The hourglass-shaped piece of linen probably tied at each hip like a string bikini. This garment was even more puzzling to experts. Who would have worn it? Men? Women? Men are usually the only ones depicted wearing this kind of garment in paintings and artwork from the Renaissance (fourteenth to seventeenth centuries). Yet purchase records from some European royal families document that women such as Maria de' Medici (1573–1642), queen of France, and Eleanor of Toledo (1522–1562), a noblewoman, owned loose-fitting underwear-like garments. Various pieces of Renaissance literature disparage women who wore such clothes, calling them prostitutes, or fallen women. History is very contradictory about underwear. Whether that's because society accepted a range of choices, some for royalty and others for average folks, or because undergarments were a forbidden topic is unclear.

THAT TIME OF THE MONTH

So, what about menstruation? Surely, medieval and Renaissance women had some way of dealing with monthly flow, but historians know very little about this. Until recently, traditional anthropology focused on men's lives and community practices without investigating women's issues such as menstruation. According to Dr. Sara Read, a lecturer at Loughborough University in England, women in many cultures practiced free bleeding—they bled into their shifts and allowed their long skirts to hide the blood. Others secluded themselves at home or in structures reserved for menstruating women. Most historians assume that women used various absorptives, such as cloth, wool, papyrus, or moss.

All the way up until the nineteenth century, bleeding into a chemise was a common reality for most women. In 1899 a female German physician, Dr. Hope Bridges Adams Lehmann, wrote, "It is completely disgusting to bleed into your chemise, and wearing that same chemise for four to eight days can cause infections." She may have been an early proponent of germ theory— the scientific discovery that germs cause disease and infection. That would explain her alarm at a centuries-old practice. Yet what options did women have? Undergarments, especially menstruation-friendly underwear and sanitary products as we know them, were not manufactured until after the Industrial Revolution of the mid-nineteenth century. The first disposable sanitary pads were produced by Southall's in 1888. Tampons came along in the 1930s, freeing many women from the awkward discomfort of thick pads. The newest innovation in menstruation appeared in 2014. A company called Thinx introduced "period-proof" panties. Each pair features several absorbent layers of fabric inside a moisture-proof outer layer. Women can free bleed into their period panties and then wash and reuse them.

Days for Girls

In the twenty-first century, women in developed nations such as the United States have easy, affordable ways for managing menstruation. However, this is not true for women in poor, developing countries. Many cultures continue to stigmatize menstruation in ways that impair women's abilities to freely move through their communities. For example, in some parts of rural Nepal, girls and women are expected to wait out their time of the month in isolated huts. In Niger menstruating women are prohibited from praying, preparing food, and getting water. Menstruation is so stigmatized in rural Niger that women can't hang sanitary rags in the sun to dry after washing. When hung inside, drying is less rapid and the cloths can become mildewed or bacteria-laden. In many parts of the world, girls and women are forced to skip work and school when they have their periods. Some girls lose up to five days of school a month.

Based near Seattle, Washington, Days for Girls is a nonprofit organization that provides girls and women in sub-Saharan Africa and Southeast Asia with free reusable sanitary kits. Each kit, in a cloth tote bag, includes a colorful fabric moisture shield that holds an absorbent, flannel liner. The kits also include underwear, a washcloth, and a resealable plastic bag for soiled liners. Teams around the world sew the kits and donate them to the project. You can get involved at DaysForGirls.org.

FIVE THOUSAND YEARS OF LOINCLOTHS

Unlike women, who were letting the breeze in for centuries, men wore underwear or something like underwear from the very beginning. One of the earliest examples comes from the five-thousand-year-old mummy known as Ötzi the Iceman. When he was discovered in 1991 in a melting glacier in the Italian Alps, his naturally mummified body provided an incredible amount of information about what his life had been like. Even down to his underwear.

Ötzi was wearing a loincloth made of narrow strips of sheep leather. They had been stitched together to make a rectangle 39 inches (100 cm) wide by 13 inches (33 cm) long. He wore it fastened between the legs with a leather belt. Instead of pants, Ötzi wore laced, thigh-high, goat-leather leg warmers that attached to the belt and a hide coat made of goat and sheepskin that fell to his thighs.

The Iceman wasn't the only one sporting a loincloth. For example, the ancient Egyptian king Tutankhamen was buried in 1323 BCE with 145 loincloths woven of linen. Ancient Chinese underwear for men were a cut-and-sewn version of this simple garment. The Roman version was called a *subligaculum*. In medieval Japan, samurai warriors wore a linen loincloth called a *fundoshi*, a garment that wasn't replaced in Japan by modern briefs until the mid-twentieth century. The men of many American Indian tribes wore animal hide loincloths often called breechclouts.

Gandhi wore a homespun dhoti to symbolize his loyalty to Indian culture. He rejected Western-style clothing as part of his effort to throw off English colonial rule in India.

In the 1930s, Indian resistance leader Mahatma Gandhi wore only a white loincloth called a dhoti when he went out in public. Gandhi was making a political statement. The dhoti represented his rejection of Western culture and showed his dedication to the poor and oppressed people he was trying to liberate through his work.

THE POWER POLITICS OF UNDERWEAR

Clothing, both underwear and outerwear, has always functioned as a visible sign of status, wealth, and power. The style of a garment, the quality of materials, the skill required to make the garment, and the presence or absence of certain elements of an outfit indicate social class, rank, and livelihood. From ancient Greece and Rome to feudal Japan to medieval and Renaissance Europe, many cultures have instituted sumptuary laws, which regulated who could wear what. For example, in Europe only the nobility could use certain fabrics or decorative features. Prostitutes were often singled out by colored armbands or other distinctive pieces of clothing. In many cultures, members of minority groups might be required to wear clothes that identified their affiliation. These complex systems of laws made people dress according to their social rank. A person caught wearing a forbidden color or type of fabric would be fined. Those fairy tales about poor girls getting ball gowns from fairy godmothers and winning the hearts of princes, were just that—fairy tales. There was no way to look more important, from a legal and social perspective, than you really were.

The absence of clothes has also been used throughout history as a means of control. For example, people in bondage in ancient Egypt, Rome, Greece, and in early America were bought and sold in slave markets. There, they were placed on display, naked, for potential buyers to inspect their bodies. In different cultures and at different times, many people in bondage—both adults and children—were also forced to work naked or nearly naked. Being unclothed in public was a mark of servility, and it dehumanized those who were unable to exercise control over their own bodies or their work.

When Gandhi wore the dhoti to public functions, he was highlighting this practice as a form of protest.

Societal expectations about what was proper or appropriate for women to wear also was a means of control. In medieval Europe, underpants and trousers were a symbol of male power. If the average woman were to wear such garments, she was considered immoral or sinfully trying to undermine her husband's authority. The nakedness of a women beneath her dress signaled sexual availability. Wives were not allowed to refuse sex with their husbands at any time for any reason.

Over time, both outerwear and underwear for women became more complex and restrictive. No longer simply meant to keep the body warm and protect clothes from sweat or blood, women's undergarments had a new function: forcing the female body into very specific shapes to satisfy a man's idea of beauty.

CHAPTER TWO

Brace Yourself

The history of clothing is a history of difference. Men have practical, functional things to wear. Women adapt to discomfort, expense, time-sucking beauty rituals, and limited mobility to look good and have a pleasing shape. Pleasing to whom? And what is pleasing anyway?

Throughout history, most societies have been patriarchal, or ruled by men and their values. Women have played a subservient, second-class role in these societies. In patriarchal cultures, men control and eroticize the female body. Most women aspire to that same image of female beauty and work hard to achieve it. The image of the ideal body has changed over the centuries, from big boobs to no boobs and back again. From an emphasis on a round belly to a flat one or from slim hips to an exaggerated bottom. Creating the right look usually requires structured undergarments and specifically designed outerwear. Changing fashions have typically driven innovations in design and been supported by new technologies.

Women through the ages have worn hundreds of different kinds of undergarments. Designers and fashion historians divide these garments into two main categories—lingerie and corsetry—based on whether their structure is soft or hard. Lingerie is soft: slips, petticoats, nightgowns, drawers, camisoles, and bras without underwire or stiffening. Many fashion historians also include hosiery, garters, nightcaps, and pocket-like bags worn underneath gowns. Corsetry is hard: corsets, bustiers, crinolines, bustles, girdles, and stiffened or underwire bras for structural support. Together, these undergarments shaped a woman's body to the styles and preferences of the time.

ROUND LIKE THE MOON

The ideal European woman in the fourteenth and fifteenth centuries had flattened, deemphasized breasts and a full, round stomach. The cut of her clothes made her look pregnant. Neither a modern-day athlete with ripped abs nor a celebrity with artificial double Ds would have been considered beautiful. Men wanted to see a body that suggested fecundity (fertility), so the focus was only on the belly.

The *Arnolfini Portrait*, painted in 1434 CE by Dutch painter Jan van Eyck (1390–1441) is a wedding portrait of Italian merchant Giovanni di Nicolao Arnolfini and his wife, Jeanne Cenami. In the painting, she is wearing a green

gown belted just below the breasts, with her hand resting on the many folds of draped fabric around her prominent belly. Underneath, Cenami is wearing a blue kirtle (a simple dress of the medieval era). Between the kirtle and her skin, Cenami was most likely wearing a linen shift, a

The *Arnolfini Portrait* by Jan van Eyck, dated 1434, shows a popular image of female beauty of the time. The wife's dress and undergarments accentuate her stomach to suggest fertility and pregnancy.

laced bodice to flatten her chest, and sewn stockings held up with ribbons or straps buckled below the knee. Her exaggerated shape depicts fertility as the ultimate goal of womankind.

SHAKE THOSE HIPS

During the sixteenth and early seventeenth centuries, all eyes were on hips or at least the pretend hips. The key to fashion success was a farthingale, a type of hooped underskirt. The structural pieces of this undergarment were made of baleen (keratin plates from the mouths of certain whales), strips of wood, or bundled reeds formed into hoops and sewn in concentric circles into a linen underskirt. The hoops of the Spanish farthingale were aligned from biggest and widest (near the floor) to smallest and narrowest (at the waist), creating an inverted cone-shape that gave the same silhouette (shape) to the dress worn over the farthingale. The French farthingale created a silhouette more like a round tabletop with the woman's torso in the middle. The hoops sewn into the underskirt were

During the reign of Queen Elizabeth I (1558–1603), the farthingale created a slim waist and an exaggerated hip line. In this portrait by Marcus Gheeraerts the Younger, the queen wears her dress over a French farthingale.

all the same diameter. The top one had interior spokes (like a wheel) that attached at the woman's waist. The higher a woman's social class, the bigger and more cumbersome the farthingale. In 1617 Queen Anne of Denmark wore a French farthingale that was 4 feet (1.2 m) wide!

Farthingales made it very hard for women to get around. Women in the middle classes, who had to work in their homes, at bakeries, or at other

Farthingales shaped the silhouette of any skirt a woman wore. The French farthingale (*left*) had spokes at the waist to extend the skirt far beyond the natural hips. The Spanish farthingale (*right*) created a less exaggerated look. Both drew attention to a woman's waist.

trades, wanted in on the hip-shaking action of fashion, but they couldn't afford to have their movements so curtailed. As a nod to the fashion of the day, they wore a bum roll instead of a farthingale. The roll was a long, cylindrical pillow tied around the waist just above the hips. The bum roll held the skirts out, but not so much that a woman lost her freedom of motion.

Another key to the Renaissance-era look was a flattened chest and cinched waist. To achieve this, a woman wore a corset that laced up the back and was often built into her dress. The corset was stiffened with stays—rigid strips of baleen, wood, bone, or ivory—sewn into the fabric of the corset. The front of the corset had a long narrow pocket of fabric that held a piece of bone or horn called a busk (1 inch, or 2.5 cm, wide) that went from between the breasts at the top, past the waist, and down to the pubic bone. Bending at the waist was pretty much impossible for a woman wearing one of these.

Servants helped noble women don their many layers of clothing each morning. First, a woman put on a linen chemise and stockings that tied under the knee. A servant would strap the farthingale in place and cover it with

many layers of embroidered petticoats. The corset and dress (sometimes separate garments but often a dress with a built-in corset) went on next. The dress was usually split in the middle of the front of the skirt to reveal a bit of the fancy petticoats

Paintings are one way researchers learn about the history of fashion. In this eighteenth-century portrait by Alexander Roslin, a woman wears an intricately designed stomacher. The triangular fabric panel accentuated a woman's cleavage and tapered her waist. Stomachers were sometimes decorated with jewels, ribbons, or an *échelle*, a series of bows down the front.

underneath. The servant laced and tied the dress and then helped the woman put on a stomacher. This fancy triangular piece of embroidered fabric fitted over the bodice (front breast section) of the dress. To finish off the look, the noblewoman might wear a frontlet (a kind of hood or bonnet) and a partlet (a fancy lacy collar). If she were a member of a royal family, she might instead choose a ruff. This elaborate starched linen neckpiece was edged in lace. Some ruffs were made entirely of lace, such as those in some classic paintings of Shakespeare.

Filling the Gap

The codpiece, a fabric or leather flap covering a man's genitalia, was a crucial piece of male attire during the fifteenth and sixteenth centuries. At first, it was fairly practical. Men's hosiery (stockings) came in two pieces, one for each leg. The codpiece, slightly padded for warmth and protection (especially when worn under armor), filled in the gap in front between the legs. When men discovered the codpiece could also be used as a pocket, the size of the codpiece increased. During the sixteenth century, the style was to pad the codpiece to excessive proportions, meant to draw the eye and emphasize the wearer's virility (sexual potency). Codpieces can still be found today as part of heavy metal performance costumes. Male baseball players wear athletic cups, which serve a function similar to that of codpieces from the Middle Ages. And by the way, *cod* was Renaissance slang for "scrotum."

Kings wore codpieces too. In this portrait of King Henry VIII of England, by Hans Holbein the Younger, the king's power and manliness is evident through his proud posture, his direct gaze, his dagger, and his codpiece.

DON'T SLOUCH, LITTLE LADY

Although the farthingale stuck around in the Spanish royal court until 1700, by 1625 it had disappeared from English fashions. It was replaced with softer, looser petticoats. The focus was no longer on the hips. Even as the women of seventeenth-century Europe were breathing a sigh of relief over their less cumbersome skirts, they signed up for a new version of fashion torture. The judging eye of fashion focused on perfect posture and blooming breasts. To achieve this look, women fortified their corsets with longer, stiffer stays. Then the upper body had very limited mobility. The corsets rose higher on the chest, pushing the breasts upward and exposing far more bosom than earlier garments. Dresses barely covered this abundance of flesh.

WATCH THE DOOR

After 1710 large skirts were back in fashion. This look was created by massive cage crinolines made of cloth-covered wicker hoops. Wearing her chemise, a woman would step into the crinoline, hoist it up over the hips, and tie it into place. Petticoats and the outer dress went on over the crinoline. Wearing one of these crinolines was like having a giant birdcage around your waist! Navigating tight spaces such as stairwells was almost impossible. Walking in a crowd was like being in a silk-covered game of bumper cars. Women had to adopt a waddling gait to maneuver in their own dresses, and men who bumped into the edges of the skirts complained of bruised shins.

By the middle of the century, panniers replaced hoops. Initially made of wicker, panniers were like inverted baskets that tied onto the body, one hanging from each hip. The panniers were strapped on over a woman's chemise and covered with a layer of petticoats. From the front, a woman's silhouette resembled a domed roof. From the side, she appeared thin and flattened. Some panniers measured 6 feet (1.8 m) across! Women scuttled through doors sideways to accommodate their immense skirts, and sitting down meant perching on the edge of chairs.

The ultrafashionable of the eighteenth century adopted a practice called tight lacing to achieve the wasp-waisted look. Corsets, worn underneath the dress, were laced as tightly as possible to cinch the waist and push the breasts upward. The tightest corsets laced in the back, and only women who could afford a maid to dress them and to pull firmly at the lacing in back could wear them. Lower-class women wore jumps, a corset often made of leather or thick cloth that was worn over the dress and laced in the front.

Once a woman was laced into her corset, tied into panniers, and layered in petticoats and a dress, attending to the needs of the body got complicated, especially in an era before indoor plumbing. When women in the eighteenth century needed to relieve themselves, a servant would bring them a portable urinal called a *bourdaloue*, a porcelain dish that looks like a gravy boat. The noblewoman would hold it in place while she urinated, a task made easier by the lack of underwear. Afterwards her servant would empty the *bourdaloue* outside.

At the end of the eighteenth century, fashion changed again. This time, the wide-hipped silhouette created by panniers was out of favor. The look of the day emphasized the bottom. Women threw their panniers in the trash heap and moved on to the bustle, a bulbous frame made of wicker and fabric. One type resembled a cage crinoline except that it only had hoops on the back side. Another type looked more like a wicker cage that perched on a woman's bottom. When covered with a petticoat with extra frills in the back and a dress, the woman looked thin from the front, but from the side, her lower half extended several feet behind her. It was easy for a woman wearing a bustle to get through doorways, but sitting down on a chair was almost impossible.

WHO DO YOU THINK YOU ARE?

Suffering for fashion was definitely part of the eighteenth-century aesthetic. Tight lacing compressed ribs and bruised flesh. Women wrote about the pain of wearing corsets and the pleasure of achieving the right look. They faced a judgment of character based on looks alone. If they didn't wear the style of the day, they were viewed negatively as poor and unfashionable. They might also be called lazy, slatternly (promiscuous), ugly, and fat. But if a lower-class woman tight-laced instead of wearing jumps, she was called uppity, vain, and whorish.

In the mid-eighteenth century, a young English woman, whose mother wouldn't allow (or couldn't afford) the tight-laced look for her daughter, committed suicide by jumping to her death rather than wear jumps. A journalist of the time ridiculed her with this pun in rhyme:

> *Women, they tell us, have strange ways,*
> *So Harriet pin'd for stiffen'd stays;*
> *Till hopeless grown, and in the dumps,*
> *For want of Stays, she took to Jumps.*

Political cartoons in daily newspapers made fun of fat women trying to get laced up. Cartoons also suggested that the tight-laced style was so erotic that men couldn't possibly control themselves around corseted women and weren't to be blamed for taking liberties.

Moral or loose? Proper or vain? No matter what they did, women couldn't win. But the ridicule and the rigid and uncomfortable clothing were effective controls on women's behavior.

This satirical illustration, thought to be by British illustrator William Heath in the 1820s, pokes fun at tight lacing. It also makes fun of mechanization as a solution for all challenges, great and small. (The tight-lacing machine was a figment of the artist's imagination.)

All the Poor Little Children

From the sixteenth to the nineteenth century, many parents believed that young bodies, if left unrestrained, would grow into twisted and bent adults. Babies of both sexes were laced into an infant version of a corset, often called a waist. Boys wore them until about the age of six. Girls were not so lucky. Physical restraint was their lot in life. They were dressed as little adults, complete with miniature corsets to "prevent deformities of the skeleton" and "procure an agreeable waist and a well-positioned bust.

For this 1669 portrait by John Michael Wright, James Cecil and his sister, Lady Catherine, were dressed in ornate outfits modeled on adult styles. As children born into English nobility, they followed the fashion of wearing corsets that forced a straightened posture.

A SAILOR'S LOVE SONG

Fashion went hand in hand with slaughter. From the mid seventeenth to the late nineteenth centuries, the whaling industry flourished around the world. The center of the whaling industry in the United States was in New Bedford, Massachusetts, a small town along the northeastern coastline. At its peak in the mid-nineteenth century, the industry employed ten thousand men and boys, who went to sea for years at a time. About two million whales were killed during the eighteenth and nineteenth centuries, and nearly three million more were killed in the twentieth century.

The industry was fueled by a hunger for whale oil (the main source of fuel for lamps) and for corset stays. The average corset required thirty to forty pieces of baleen to uplift the breasts and squeeze in the stomach. For the women who could afford it, baleen was far superior to wood, reeds, bone, or wicker. Baleen was firm yet very flexible. It was easy to cut and shape, and once set into a corset, baleen stays held their shape well.

In 1851 American writer Herman Melville published the classic novel *Moby-Dick,* a gore-filled description of life aboard a whaling vessel, based on his own experience at sea. The decks streamed with blood. Boiling oil from the heads of sperm whales filled the air with greasy black smoke. Sharks snapped and crunched at carcasses slung over the sides of the ship. It was a gruesome business. When whalers weren't processing the carcasses of slaughtered whales, they spent their downtime carving love notes into flattened strips of whale bone. Upon returning home, a sailor would give his carving, known as scrimshaw, to the woman he loved to use as a corset busk (or busque). Every morning, when the woman slid the busk into the fabric of her corset, she was slipping a token of her lover's affection between her breasts.

These colorful, decorative busks from the nineteenth century were carved from whalebone. They are on display at the New Bedford Whaling Museum.

The whaling industry began to decline toward the end of the nineteenth century because of the discovery of petroleum. This resource replaced whale oil in lamps.

It was a crisis for corsetry. By then, however, the Industrial Revolution had brought steel and mass manufacturing to the Western world. And from then on, stainless steel was the material of choice for women's corset stays.

CHAPTER THREE

Nineteenth-Century Upheaval

In the twenty-first century, it's called fast fashion. A new design shows up on the runways in Paris and New York. A few months later, it's at upscale clothing stores for astronomical prices. A few months after that, the knockoffs show up at Zara, Target, and H&M. Six months after the first fashion show, designers launch their new lines, and the churning cycle of fast fashion begins again.

Styles didn't change quite that rapidly in the nineteenth century but almost. High waistlines and flowing skirts. Tight lacing and layered petticoats. Low-cut gowns. High-cut gowns. Huge, puffy leg-of-mutton sleeves resembling giant fabric balloons. Bustles and corsets to force the hourglass figure. Every few years, high-society style changed and the look of the female body changed with it.

The underlying garments that supported each new look were all modifications of basic corsetry. Yet underneath those stiff stays and layers of linen, something far more revolutionary was happening. And it was raising hackles throughout American and European societies.

PRETTIES AND KNICKERS

Up until the nineteenth century, underpants were definitely the least important part of a woman's underclothing. In the twenty-first century, most of us wouldn't feel completely dressed without a pair of unders. Back then, things were very different. Usually the ladies went commando. But sometimes women wore loose-fitting pants called drawers.

Drawers looked like loose shorts or pants, and they were made of soft fabric such as linen or cotton. Sometimes the legs of the drawers hung straight down. Other styles were gathered at the knee or ankle with a ribbon inserted into the seam. They weren't girly versions of boxer shorts. Oh no! These old-time drawers all had one very important feature in common: an open crotch.

Each pair of bifurcated (split) drawers had an open seam between the legs so that it was easier to go to the bathroom—and this is where the revolution was under way. Actresses and dancers, like those at the Moulin Rouge in Paris, decided to sew those babies shut. It made a lot of sense. These women were onstage, strutting their stuff, and the last thing they wanted was to flash the men in the audience. But actresses and dancers were not considered respectable ladies. In fact, they were lumped together with prostitutes in the unsavory category. Ironically, the sewed-up undergarments, which concealed a woman's genitals, became erotic and therefore scandalous.

This 1767 painting, *The Swing*, by Jean-Honoré Fragonard, depicts an onlooker peeking at the woman's exposed drawers. During this era, drawers would have had an open crotch, so the painting was actually quite racy.

In 1856 a technological marvel—the sprung-steel hoopskirt—appeared on the fashion scene. It was lightweight and bouncy, unlike the enormously heavy cage crinolines of earlier decades. It could be mass-produced in factories and so was more affordable than a one-of-a-kind handmade piece. While these hoops were magnificent at creating the bell shape that women wanted, they weren't stable. The steel hoops could fly up and reveal what was underneath. If you were wearing open-crotch drawers, that meant everything!

You'd think that the solutions would have been pretty obvious—either give up those hoops or close up the drawers. But change is never straightforward. Doctors debated whether open-crotch drawers offered healthful ventilation of the lady parts or introduced germs.

This photograph from 1860 shows a woman wearing a cage crinoline. The photo is from a series of comic French photographs showing the elaborate routine behind dressing to suit the fashion of the era.

Unlocking the Chastity Belt

In a pivotal scene in the movie *Mad Max: Fury Road* (2015), the five wives of Immortan Joe remove their toothed, metal chastity belts with a bolt cutter. These locked garments were intended to prevent sexual activity. The symbolism in the movie is clear: these women, with the help of female warrior Imperator Furiosa, are breaking free from forced marriage and sexual imprisonment.

Historians believe that this German chastity belt from the seventeenth or eighteenth century was fairly comfortable. Even though the belt and clasps at the waist are iron, the garment was lined with linen and was well cushioned. Experts therefore think the belt was not meant for punishment for immoral sexual behavior. They think it was probably a garment women wore voluntarily as protection from unwanted sexual advances while traveling or in other risky situations.

Stories about chastity belts have been around for centuries, but historians aren't quite sure if they were ever really used very much. Some experts think these locked, metal underwear would have caused injury to the wearer and were also impractical. How would a woman go to the bathroom? Some museum collections display devices labeled as chastity belts, but historians suspect that many were actually used for torturing women and not for protecting their virginity. Early European literature and paintings refer to the "belt of Venus" (the goddess of love) or to "girdles of chastity." But scholars think this might have been symbolic language, not literal, just as the key to someone's heart is not an actual key.

During the nineteenth century, however, Americans and Europeans could purchase locking metal undergarments from catalogs. Adult women sometimes wore them when going out in public as rape prevention devices. Husbands sometimes insisted women wear them to ensure sexual fidelity. Parents put them on both male and female children to prevent masturbation, which was considered sinful.

Moralists were adamant that open-crotch drawers made a woman too available for sex. Lewd cartoons in newspapers showed men getting an eyeful when women stumbled in the streets and their hoops flew up. In the 1860s, an article in an English fashion magazine advised that "drawers should be trimmed with frills." After all, if men were going to get glimpses of the unmentionables, what they saw should be frilly, soft, and feminine.

But why was it such a big deal for women to wear closed-crotch drawers? Was society afraid of women in pants?

DEVIANT WOMEN

Gender distinctions are reinforced through clothing. In the nineteenth century, young girls wore dresses with short, closed-crotch pantalets underneath. These were outerwear not underwear and looked a little like modern baby clothes with a frilled bottom. Young boys wore knee-length breeches. A change of costume marked the transition to adulthood. Men wore trousers. Women wore long dresses. But a growing number of European and American women wanted practical clothing so they could conduct daily activities unencumbered. They wanted to ride bicycles and participate in other sports without getting tangled in their skirts.

In 1851 Elizabeth Smith Miller from Geneva, New York, came up with a new look consisting of billowy trousers (sometimes called Turkish trousers because they resembled a garment worn by Turkish men). They were to be worn underneath a dress that hung to mid-calf. Amelia Jenks Bloomer promoted the newfangled outfit in her magazine the *Lily*, and it was called the bloomer costume or the "American Dress." In Bloomer's opinion, "When you find a burden in belief or apparel, cast it off."

The public outcry was intense. Look at her ankles! She looks like a man! Crisis!

The bigger issue was that the majority of the women who adopted the bloomer costume were also part of the women's rights movement. These women were fighting for the right to vote, for greater access to education, and for increased economic opportunities. Much of mainstream society was in chaos at the idea that women would gain rights that had been reserved for men. In 1851 the editorial board of the *New York Times* wrote: "We regret to see how obstinately our American women are bent on appropriating [taking over] more than their fair share of Constitutional privileges. . . . There is an obvious tendency to encroach upon [take over] masculine manners . . . which cannot be too severely rebuked [criticized] or too speedily repressed."

Women who wore bloomers were accused of being loose and immoral. They were also said to be anti-male—a code word for lesbians, and homosexuality was deep, deep, deep in the American closet. Cartoons depicted bloomer-wearing women as grotesquely masculine—smoking cigars (women didn't smoke in public in those days), using walking sticks (a male

This 1851 illustration by American artist Nathaniel Currier shows the bloomer costume. Elizabeth Smith Miller is credited with creating bloomers when she was gardening in her cumbersome floor-length skirt. In frustration she cut her skirt with a scissors.

fashion item), and proposing marriage to effeminate baby-men. Women who wore the bloomer costume were viewed as hysterical, deviant (another code word for lesbianism), and criminal.

The pressure was so intense that most women gave up their bloomers and went back to traditional, feminized clothing. Nonetheless, Lydia Sayer Hasbrouck and other American dress reform proponents founded the National Dress Reform Association in the United States in 1856, and Lady Florence Harberton and Emily King founded the Rational Dress Society in England in 1881. Both organizations fought for a woman's right to wear comfortable, practical clothing. They also suggested that the total weight of a woman's undergarments should be under 7 pounds (3 kg)! Many wanted to eliminate corsets because these garments were so restrictive. Advocates of dress reform in the United States continued to be important voices in the women's rights movement of the nineteenth century.

THE POLITICS OF POCKETS

Bloomers weren't the only thing making waves. Believe it or not, the lowly pocket was the subject of heated debate in the nineteenth century.

In the medieval era, no one had pockets. Instead, both sexes stashed their necessities in bags secured at the hip with a belt—the earliest fanny packs! In the late seventeenth century, the first sewn-in pockets appeared in men's coats, vests, and pants. Women had no such luck. Their fanny packs were swapped out for cloth bags that hung from the waist underneath their skirts and petticoats. Into these bags, women stashed everything from perfume to snuffboxes, smelling salts to sewing kits. To get their items, women slipped their hands through discreet slits in the sides of their skirts. These "pockets" were fashionable through the mid-eighteenth century.

When fashions grew more streamlined in the mid to late eighteenth century, these hanging bags gave way to reticules—small, decorated purses with a drawstring to pull tight as the closure. While this might sound better than having a heavy bag whacking your legs at every step, it actually reduced a woman's privacy. Because carrying a purse was more visible than the hidden cloth bags of previous decades, women, especially those involved in the revolutionary movement sweeping France in the late eighteenth century, could no longer easily and discreetly carry personal or political secrets.

Women's desire for pockets expanded during the nineteenth century, and dress reformers advocated for pockets in everyday wear. But opposition to pockets in women's clothing was just as fierce as it had been to the bloomer costume. Pockets were considered masculine attire. The sight of a woman wearing clothes with pockets and walking with her hands in those pockets was considered a shocking outrage. Like women in bloomers, women using pockets were labeled deviant.

This Venetian reticule is a modern re-creation of a ladies' reticule. Because pockets were considered unladylike for many decades, women looked for other convenient ways to carry their personal items.

In a *New York Times* essay ridiculing dress reformers and suffragettes (women who advocated for women's right to vote), one man wrote, "No pocketless people has ever been great since pockets were invented, and the female sex cannot rival us [men] while it is pocketless." As women gained more political rights over the decades, they eventually gained more freedom of dress. Yet the fight for pockets lingered into the twentieth century. In 1954 French designer Christian Dior claimed that "men have pockets to keep things in, women for decoration."

A SHOCKING SHADE OF PALE BLUE

Walk into a modern lingerie store and you can buy underwear in a rainbow of colors and a multitude of patterns. It would be a pretty boring shopping day to come home with nothing but white and black.

Not so in the nineteenth century. Most undergarments for men and women were the natural, off-white color of sun-bleached linen and had been for centuries. It was a color associated with modesty and purity. The other acceptable color for women's undergarments was dark gray, which signified that the wearer was morally upright. Only prostitutes wore corsets or shifts in other colors.

Rich, complex color palettes were part of impressionism, a new and radical style of painting that swept Europe in the mid to late nineteenth century. These artists used their work to represent real life, not idealized versions of it. For their subjects, impressionist painters chose street scenes and people who were shunned by mainstream society. One such painter was Frenchman Édouard Manet. His 1877 painting *Nana* sent shock waves through European society. It depicts a courtesan putting on her makeup while her next client, a gentleman, watches her from the edge of the scene. Nana is wearing a white linen chemise and a pale blue corset. Viewers recognized

Édouard Manet's famous painting *Nana* depicts a French prostitute in a colorful corset. Originally viewed as a shocking image, it eventually created a fashion trend for lingerie in colors besides modest white.

Nana as a prostitute through her colorful corset and also her name, a common one for prostitutes in France.

To the modern eye, there is nothing salacious or indecent about Nana. She is wearing far more clothes than the average Victoria's Secret lingerie model. But in the nineteenth century, Parisian commentators called the painting shameless and brazen. One newspaper printed an anonymous editorial rebuke of the artwork, saying, "More than nude, in her chemise, the *fille* [girl] shows off."

So the truly scandalous thing about the painting is that Nana is not ashamed of herself. Nana, not her gentleman caller, is at the center of the story, and Nana is looking straight at the viewer with a calm, straightforward expression. No one at the time wanted to discuss prostitution openly or acknowledge that a young woman could express sexuality without shame. The newspaper concluded, "She is sordid one hundred times over, this whore."

By the end of the nineteenth century, however, more and more women of all social classes were wearing colorful body linens. Initially women began wearing pale pink and the very same blue that got Nana into so much trouble. Over time, acceptable colors became bolder and more vibrant, ranging from indigo to magenta.

Lace Me Up

Long before the word *corset* came into common use in English at the end of the eighteenth century, women wore undergarments reinforced with stiff strips of baleen (often called whalebone even though it wasn't actually bone), wood, or bone. Depending on the region and time period, these garments were called busques, stays (which could also refer to the stiffening in the corset), *corps à baleine* (literally "body of whale" in French), jumps, or bodies. Corsets that came in two halves to be laced together were sometimes called *a pair of bodies*. The term *corset* comes from the Latin word *corpus*, which means "body."

ELECTRIFIED, ATHLETIC, AND EROTIC

During the Victorian era, when Queen Victoria ruled Britain (1837–1901), social change was afoot. Both Europeans and Americans were debating open- versus closed-crotch drawers, pockets for women, the bloomer costume, and colorful undergarments. The corset was also controversial. Not wearing a corset was unacceptable, but wearing a corset the wrong way or for the wrong reasons was also unacceptable. For example, arguments raged about how tightly a corset should be laced and what kind of fabric it should be made of.

Hucksters promised good health to women who bought and wore corsets with metal stays that had been treated with electric pulses during manufacturing. Dr. Gustav Jaeger thought that cotton gave off poisonous vegetable gases and that silk was nothing more than worm poop in thread form. His innovation was wool corsets, which he said had "all the advantages of girded loins [physical support] without the disadvantages [of unhealthy materials]."

Suffragettes and other women wanted more comfort and flexibility from their undergarments so they could ride bicycles and participate in sports with ease. Other

A magazine ad from 1887 claims health and beauty for the customer who sports Dr. Scott's electric corset. The bogus electric corset contained magnets that promised to cure a range of diseases and discomforts. However, corsets were themselves a cause of many problems, including fainting and compressed ribs and internal body organs.

A List of Corset Horrors

In 1874 Luke Limner published *Madre Natura versus the Moloch of Fashion: A Social Essay,* which contained a list of ninety-seven "diseases produced by stays and corsets according to the testimony of eminent medical men." These diseases included:

head pain

shortened life span

seizure

asthma

tuberculosis

cough

fainting

hemorrhoids

hunchback

hysteria

difficulty breathing

deformed nipples

lung failure

stomach pain

swollen feet

cancer

sterility

and . . . ugly children. (Yes, this was really on the list!)

women wanted to be laced as tightly as possible since the ideal Victorian fashion was for a woman to be fleshy and soft on the top and wasp-waisted in the middle. Tight lacing to achieve an extremely small waist (under 16 inches, or 41 cm) was also considered sexy by some people.

Both medical doctors and quacks debated how tight was too tight. They documented corset-related medical (or pseudomedical) problems, such as reduced lung capacity, fainting, and compressed ribs and internal organs. Some claimed that women who wore corsets lost strength in their backs and stomach muscles. Others insisted that the opposite was true: without a corset, a woman would become hunched and immobile. Everyone had an opinion.

CHAPTER FOUR

Innovation and Invention

After the Victorian era, King Edward VII became Britain's reigning monarch, and the years of his rule (1901-1910) are known as the Edwardian era. It was characterized by massive social, technological, and economic upheaval in American and European society. As cities grew larger and citizens intermingled, class distinctions began to crumble. Social mores changed. Some women continued to demand equal rights. Others were clinging to rigid, traditional values of earlier times. This clash of new and old, combined with technological and manufacturing advances, created an explosion of change in women's undergarments. Innovation and invention were the sign of the times.

A PASSION FOR PEDDLING

One of the most liberating inventions for women was the bicycle. The cycling craze really got cranking in the 1890s and continued into the twentieth century. Suddenly European and American women could go where they wanted—without a male chaperone. As long as they had something to wear that was comfortable, they could move about unconstrained. These athletically minded young women wore a shorter and looser corset, sometimes called a waist, in which it was much easier to peddle and to breathe. They asked their tailors to add pockets to their cycling costumes so they could carry personal belongings easily. And since these cyclists were often alone, they also had tailors add leather-lined pockets designed to discreetly carry pistols for protection.

Ice-skating, gymnastics, tennis, skiing, and horseback riding became popular among women, and they needed comfortable clothes to participate. Suddenly divided skirts called culottes and knickerbockers (baggy trousers) were popular, even if rejected by high fashion. Women who liked to swim didn't want to struggle in the water weighted down by yards of fabric skirts. In 1907 Australian swimmer Annette Kellerman (1887–1975) was arrested in Boston, Massachusetts, for wearing a boy's bathing suit over tights. Her body was covered but not concealed. Apparently that was too much for citizens to handle! Kellerman, however, was unfazed. She went on to tour in mermaid stage shows, pioneered what is called synchronized swimming, and was the first woman to appear fully nude in a movie, *A Daughter of the Gods*, in 1916. Other female swimmers followed her lead. Soon many women were wearing bathing suits that clung to the body and looked something like a tank top sewn to a pair of knee-length shorts.

Annette Kellerman in her famous one-piece swimsuit. Her choice was viewed as scandalous because it revealed the true shape of her body.

THE GIBSON GIRL

In spite of the successes of the rational dress movement in liberating women from restrictive corsets during sports, mainstream style was as constrictive and uncomfortable as ever. In the Edwardian era, the ideal woman was the Gibson Girl, portrayed in pen-and-ink drawings by American artist Charles Gibson. She was a blend of all that high society considered beautiful at the time: pale white skin, delicate features, a rosebud mouth, hair loosely piled upon her head, and the distinctive hourglass figure created by a specialized corset.

The Gibson Girl corset had an extra-long central busk that went from the pubic bone to just under the breasts. When tightly cinched, it pushed the chest forward and the rear backward. From the side, the woman had a distinct S-shaped form. The breasts themselves were unsupported, and women used various pads and shapers called corset covers, which were made of stays and fabric, to give the bosom a smooth, forward-jutting silhouette known as the monobosom.

The Gibson Girl was often depicted in art and advertisements cycling, golfing, or participating in other athletic events. She was supposed to represent a healthy yet modest woman, who showed no sign of exertion, never perspiring and with never more than a wisp of hair out of place. Yet it's doubtful a real Gibson Girl could

Charles Gibson drew his illustrations from real-life models, including Camille Clifford (*above*), a Danish-born actress. The Gibson Girl represented the era's female ideal: a more athletic and self-possessed woman. However, the tight corset and exposed bust did not actually encourage strenuous sporting activity.

actually have done any of those activities wearing the type of corset that was worn then.

For a brief period around 1910, the corset metamorphosed one more time. The dramatic S-shape vanished. The latest dress styles were long and slim. Corsets lengthened to accommodate the fashion, and the Gibson Girl was gone.

BIRTH OF THE BRA

The corset too, as an everyday piece of apparel, was on its way out. Back in 1889 at the Grand Exhibition in Paris, French lingerie designer Herminie Cadolle had displayed a patented garment she called the *corselet-gorge.* Basically, this was a corset cut in half to form a top piece with shoulder straps to support the breasts and a bottom piece to shape the waist. Later, she sold the top half by itself at her lingerie shop in Paris, calling this early bra *le bien-être,* or the "well-being." By 1905 the shop was selling it as the *soutien-gorge,* which translates as "breast supporter." In 1905 Cadolle made a spectacular metal bra for Mata Hari (1876–1917), a Dutch exotic dancer and courtesan who was also a spy for the French government. Herminie Cadolle's high-end lingerie company, called Cadolle, still exists and is run by Poupie Cadolle, the great-granddaughter of Herminie Cadolle. Each piece of lingerie is custom-made and finished

Dutch exotic dancer and courtesan Mata Hari (*above*) wears a metal bra designed by Herminie Cadolle. Cadolle began calling her bras *soutiens-gorge,* which is the word still used for "bra" in the French language.

by hand, which takes up to thirty hours. Cadolle even made the sexy black corset that Monica Bellucci wore in the 2015 James Bond movie *Spectre*.

Another woman who claimed to be the inventor of the bra was American socialite Mary Phelps Jacob (who later changed her name to Caresse Crosby). In 1913, when she was twenty-two years old, she was getting ready for a high-society party. As was the style, she laced into her corset, which ended under the breasts, and put on a stiff, laced upper garment called a corset cover. She recalled that it was "a box-like armour of whalebone and pink cordage," and it showed through the sheer fabric of her evening gown. Struck by inspiration, she and her maid quickly sewed together two lightweight silk pocket handkerchiefs and some pink ribbon to form a delicate backless undergarment that covered and contained Crosby's breasts. She said that it was "delicious" to wear. Crosby could dance with abandon. At the party, other young women commented on how smoothly her gown fitted. Crosby showed them her invention, and all of her friends wanted one. So Crosby started sewing. Eventually total strangers were offering to buy Crosby's bras for one dollar apiece. Crosby patented her "backless brassiere" in 1914—the first bra patent in the United States—and eventually sold the design to Warner Brothers Corset Company for $1,500. In her 1953 autobiography, *The Passionate Years*, Crosby wrote, "I can't say the brassiere will ever take as great a place in history as the steamboat, but I did invent it."

THE FASHIONS OF WAR

Everything changed with the eruption of World War I (1914–1918) in Europe. American and European women took jobs in munitions (weapons) factories and served as railway guards, firefighters, bus and train conductors, police officers, and military nurses. Many of these jobs could not be done well or easily in dresses, so women began to wear trousers regularly for the first time. The calf- or knee-length, open-crotch drawers that women had been wearing didn't work well under pants. So women began to wear shorter, closed-crotched drawers—known as knickers, or step-ins. These were the precursors of modern underwear.

In 1917, after the United States joined the war, American financier Bernard Baruch became the chairman of the War Industries Board and oversaw the purchase of war supplies. To make battleships and other equipment, US manufacturers needed as much steel as possible. Baruch knew that corset stays were made from steel, so he made a desperate plea to American women: stop wearing corsets! Thanks to the women who unlaced for the cause, the military was able to collect enough steel to build an entire battleship—28,000 tons (25,401 t)!

But women were not accustomed or inclined to go completely without supportive undergarments. They began wearing the newfangled bras. To contain and flatten their stomachs, thighs, and bottoms, women turned to a brand-new garment. The girdle was a one-piece, tube-shaped undergarment that sheathed a woman's body from under the breasts to mid-thigh. The girdle was made possible by the invention of elastic fabrics. A new manufacturing technique turned latex sap from trees into stretchy rubber. Rubber could be made into a wide range of products from tires for cars to sneaker soles to elastic for clothing. Elastic materials were relatively inexpensive, and they eliminated the need for laces in lingerie. A woman could slip on her girdle and have flexibility and ease of motion.

After the invention of the girdle, another brand-new kind of lingerie called camiknickers came on the scene. This was a one-piece combination of a bra-like top

One-piece camiknickers were popular during the Jazz Age. They created a smooth silhouette under the lighter, looser-fitting dresses of the era.

called a camisole and the new, short knickers women had been wearing. Camiknickers were perfect under the new girdles because they eliminated the gap between bra and underwear. The combination of girdle and camiknickers was also perfectly suited to the new fashions of the 1920s.

THE JAZZ AGE

The ideal woman of the 1920s was slim and small-breasted, almost boyish in her appearance. The so-called It Girl of the 1920s was movie star Clara Bow. She was tiny, perfect for the sleek styles of the day. Women wore barely there sheath dresses of delicate materials. The new elastic girdles, also known as belts, created a smooth silhouette under the fashionable dresses of the time.

And could you dance! This was the Jazz Age, when men and women tossed aside convention. Americans and Europeans had been through a brutal war and wanted to forget the suffering. Women cut their hair short—and shortened their hemlines. Men got rid of their three-piece suits and chose wide-legged baggy pants, sporty jackets, and belts instead of suspenders. And everyone, it seemed, was dancing to the edgy jazz tunes of black musicians. With shorter skirts and less restrictive undergarments, women could compete for days, if not weeks, in the popular dance marathon competitions that were all the rage.

THE GREAT DEPRESSION

When a massive stock market crash triggered the Great Depression (1929–1942), the frivolity of the Jazz Age fizzled and was replaced by desperation. Industry ground to a halt. Half of the banks in the United States failed. Millions were out of work. Trying to find a job replaced attending dance competitions. Art historian Carmenita Higginbotham says that Walt Disney's character Snow White from the movie *Snow White and the Seven Dwarves* (1937) embodied the ideal woman of 1930s culture. Snow White was pretty but humble and willing to work hard, which reflected the growing number of women trying to find ways to support their families.

Knickers were replaced with panties that look pretty much like what women and girls of the twenty-first century wear. These tight-fitting garments were possible because of the same elasticized fabrics that allowed the girdle to replace the corset. Bras were also mainstream. Husband-and-wife team William and Ida Rosenthal started the Maiden Form Brassiere Company (now Maidenform) in 1929 and introduced the cup-sizing system. Warner Bra, a competing company, took the letter-based sizing system and started calling its lingerie line Alphabet Bras.

In 1938 *Time* magazine wrote that twenty-year-old model June Cox, with her "round, high bosom . . . slim but not wasp-like waist, and gently rounded hips," was the ideal woman of the year. Instead of the boyish look of Jazz Age flappers,

In 1938 *Time* magazine featured twenty-year-old June Cox in a one-piece swimsuit as an example of the perfect female figure. The article details her curves, straight lines, and various body measurements.

the ideal woman was gentle, romantic, and hopeful, sentiments in short supply during the Depression.

In September 1939, *Vogue* magazine published an iconic image by photographer Horst P. Horst. Viewed from the back, the model's body twists in a sinuous curve. The long ribbons of her white corset drape elegantly around her, coming unlaced as if she is preparing for a romantic encounter. The image communicated elegant sexuality and erotic femininity. It also captured a fundamental change in the role of the corset in the lives of women. Corsets hadn't vanished, but they had stopped being a staple garment of everyday wear. By the 1930s, corsets were for bedrooms, not for wearing to work. This had a profound impact on the lingerie industry.

CHAPTER FIVE

Bombers and Bombshells

Betty Boop bats her huge, lash-fringed, oval eyes and purses her tiny bow-shaped mouth. Her hips waggle. Her arms flap. Her body, clad in a short dress, high heels, a garter belt, and a low-cut bodice, shimmies as she sings in a squeaky voice, punctuating every line with her signature boop-oop-a-doop catchphrase. Born in the 1930s, cartoon character Betty Boop had a profound impact on pop culture. She was distinctly female and highly sexualized. Betty Boop cartoons took on adult themes such as sexual harassment, female sexual power, drug abuse, and racism. At the time, Betty Boop was scandalous.

Her creator, Max Fleischer, based Betty Boop on white singer and actress Helen Kane. He modeled the character's appearance, boop-oop-a-doop catchphrase, and famous song "I Wanna Be Loved by You" on Kane's stage performances. What he didn't realize was that Kane had stolen the style, look, and unique riff from 1920s black jazz singer Esther Jones, known as Baby Esther. The truth came out when Kane sued Fleischer for exploiting her image. During the trial, a 1928 audio recording of Baby Esther singing the famous boop-oop-a-doop phrase confirmed that Kane had taken Baby Esther's work and called it her own. The suit against Fleischer was dismissed, and Betty Boop claimed her place in the pantheon of iconic female images.

BETTY BOOP GOES TO WAR

In 1939 Germany invaded Poland, plunging Europe into World War II (1939–1945). The roar of bomber engines cut across dark night skies. Bombs exploded over cities and farms. The United States, still recovering from the turmoil and desperation of the Great Depression, watched and waited as fighting spread across the European continent. Ground troops fought in the Netherlands, Belgium, Luxembourg, and France. Italy joined Germany, while Britain and its European allies (known as the Allies) opposed them on land and in the air. By 1940 Japan had joined Germany to fight the Allies, and in 1941, Japan's attack on Pearl Harbor, Hawaii, pushed the United States to join the Allies.

The sexuality of iconic cartoon figure Betty Boop is made obvious through her very visible garter belt, short skirts, tight bodice, and high heels.

Airpower was a critical part of the Allied strategy in Europe and in the Pacific, where the Allies fought Japanese forces. World War II was a brutal and deadly conflict. To boost morale, artists such as Don Allen, a young soldier from Rocky River, Ohio, who had graduated from the Cleveland Institute of Art, painted images of sexy women on the sides of fighter planes and bombers. Airplane nose art often included the slogan and symbol of a squadron's members. It was a way to lift the men's spirits and keep them connected to one another.

Painted images of Betty Boop shaking her hips appeared on many airplanes as did more realistic images of buxom women in lingerie—known as bombshells. Describing gorgeous women this way seems to have originated among GIs in World War I. The term took hold after American actress Jean Harlow, the original blond bombshell, starred in a 1933 movie of the same name. In World War II nose art, bombshells were depicted in body-hugging garments, slinky negligees (sheer nightgowns), bras and underwear, silk robes falling open, or completely naked. They posed astride bombs with come-hither looks. The sexualized thrill of the imagery was the "reward" for the bravery of American soldiers.

VA-VA-VOOM

From Betty Boop to nose art women, the age of the bombshell took center stage in the 1950s. The most famous woman of the decade was the actress and model Marilyn Monroe (1926–1962). Everything about her screamed sex and sensuality. She was all curves from her blond waves to her full breasts and ample hips—the new "ideal" woman. The key to achieving this voluptuous look was twofold: a highly-structured garment called a torpedo (or bullet) bra that caused the breasts to jut outward and into prominent points and a narrow, laced garment called a waspie that cinched in the waist. Decades later, in the movie *Austin Powers: International Man of Mystery* (1997), dangerous blond fembots in silver bikinis parodied the classic bullet bra. Their shiny, pointy bras shot bullets out of the nipple region.

Sam Shaw took a series of famous photographs of movie star Marilyn Monroe during the filming of *The Seven Year Itch* in 1954. Posing on top of a New York City subway grate, she holds down her skirt as gusts of air blow from below. Monroe remains an icon of American female sex appeal.

Marilyn Monroe and other bombshells of the 1950s influenced a radical shift in lingerie advertising and marketing to average women. The earliest corset advertisements from the nineteenth century, for example, were in the back of ladies' magazines. They were discreet pen-and-ink drawings with a two-dimensional depiction of the garment—the female form was not shown. In the early twentieth century, the *Saturday Evening Post* ran elegant oil paintings that advertised men's and women's undergarments, focusing on their practical use. By 1930 advertisers were using three-dimensional drawings of corsets shaped over seductive, hard-to-see, featureless female forms. Even though no flesh was revealed, the intended effect was to encourage the mind to "fill in the blanks." In the late 1940s and 1950s, glossy full-figure photos of buxom Hollywood superstars such as Jane Russell and Betty Grable were used to sell everything from Coca-Cola to cigarettes to lingerie. Advertisers had shifted the focus away from discreet functionality and toward glamour, youth, and sex appeal.

In the 1950s, Maidenform was one of the largest lingerie manufacturers in the United States. The company launched one of the most famous bra campaigns in advertising history, with its "I dreamed" ads. With illustrations and eventually photographs, the ads placed women wearing Maidenform bras in a variety of settings, some ordinary though many fantastical. The successful ads purposely linked underwear with fantasies, revealing the secret inner lives of so-called stereotypical housewives. The ads featured women and their bras in the Wild West, at the opera, on flying carpets, and at construction sites. These ads hinted at the new dual role of lingerie—to make

> Bombshells of the 1950s influenced a radical shift in lingerie advertising. . . . [It] shifted . . . away from discreet functionality . . . toward glamour, youth, and sex appeal.

I dreamed I was a knockout
in my *maidenform bra*

Arabesque*...new Maidenform bra...has bias-cut center-of-attraction for superb
separation...insert of elastic for comfort...floral circular stitching for the most beautiful contours!

White in A, B, C cups, just 2.50. Also pre-shaped (light foam lining) 3.50.

The idea for Maidenform ads showing women "dreaming" themselves into exciting and nontraditional situations came from a female copywriter.

a woman feel great, adventurous, and fun—and to make her man think she was sexy.

Movies also played a big role in making sexy lingerie appealing to mainstream society. For example, in the movie *The Merry Widow* (1952), leading lady Lana Turner wears several different frilly, laced-edged corsets, which came to be called merry widows. The 1956 movie *Baby Doll* contains footage of lead actress Carroll Baker in a flowing nightgown that barely grazes the tops of her thighs. It came to be called, you guessed it, the baby doll.

YET ANOTHER FASHION CYCLE

Lesley Lawson was the complete opposite of Marilyn Monroe. She had short hair and long, sticklike limbs. Where Monroe had curves, Lawson had angles. If Monroe was ultrafeminine, Lawson was androgynous (gender neutral). This English model, who captured the look of the new ideal woman of the 1960s, was known as Twiggy. With almost no bust, she didn't need the stiff support of torpedo bras.

Echoing the boyish figures and slim-fitting, lightweight gowns of the 1920s, clothing of the 1960s became more minimalistic. Twiggy and women built like her wore the sheer, unstructured No-Bra Bra designed by Rudi Gernreich in 1964. The focus was on comfort and functionality.

Way beyond Tighty-Whities

Men's underwear was never as complicated as women's. For much of history, men wore loincloths or loose linen underwear known as drawers. Then, in 1935, Y-front Jockey briefs, which combined a jock strap (athletic supporter) and a brief (men's version of underpants), were invented. After World War II, boxer shorts, originally modeled after the shorts worn by prizefighters in the ring, got more comfortable with the addition of the panel seat. Winston Churchill (1874–1965), a prime minister of the United Kingdom in the mid-twentieth century, liked silk boxers in a delicate shade of pale pink. But mostly, men wore practical unders in white and other masculinized colors.

The rainbow revolution in men's underwear got rolling in the 1950s with the introduction of smaller, tighter briefs in bright colors and patterns. Initially, sales were to the gay community, but this fashion accessory eventually went mainstream. In the 1977 movie *Saturday Night Fever*, John Travolta made history as the first actor to appear on-screen in tight-fitting black bikini briefs. As a result, many heterosexual men began to wear them.

Ads for men's underwear avoided the lure of sex appeal until designer Calvin Klein launched a revolutionary ad campaign in 1982. Tom Hintnaus, a 6 foot 3 (1.9 m) Olympic pole vaulter, modeled for a Calvin Klein underwear photo shoot in Greece.

The image of his bronzed, muscled body clad only in a pair of tighty-whities towered above Times Square in New York City on a massive billboard. There was no escaping the chiseled angles of his body or the bulge in his underwear. The image launched a luxury market for men's high-end designer underwear in all shapes and styles from boxers to thongs.

Pedestrians in Times Square pass underneath a giant Calvin Klein billboard. The revealing photo was revolutionary for men's underwear advertising at the time.

During the women's rights movement of the 1960s and 1970s, women openly protested the constrictions of their underwear. Here, a San Francisco protester removes her bra in front of a crowd of ogling men.

Some women in the women's rights movement of the 1960s (a movement demanding political, economic, and social equality for all people) rejected bras altogether. They associated the constricting garments with the social and political confines of patriarchy. The choice to go braless was sometimes called bra burning even though more bras were thrown away than actually burned in fiery protests.

Nonetheless, even with the gains of the feminist movement, the shape of the ideal woman's body in US society continued to cycle rapidly. The 1970s and 1980s were characterized by actresses and models such as Farah Fawcett and Cindy Crawford, who were fit and toned while also feminine. The decade of the 1990s ushered in heroin chic, a look exemplified by people with superthin bony bodies and pale skin. Famous heroin addicts, such as the musician Kurt Cobain from Nirvana, and movies such as *Trainspotting* (1996) romanticized the dangerous drug and the physical emaciation (wasting) of addicts. Designer Calvin Klein was criticized for featuring waifish model Kate Moss—who was 5 foot 7 (1.7 m) tall yet weighed only 104 pounds (47 kg)—in underwear ads.

Increasingly, the look of the ideal woman was impossible to achieve with undergarments alone. To get the right look, women turned to rigorous exercise programs such as the workout videos of actress Jane Fonda. Or they turned to plastic surgery to add to or reduce their natural shape. Even so, the gap between the average American woman's body and the ideal woman grew larger with every decade.

Comparing Body Mass Index (BMI) of "Ideal Women" to Average Women

Body mass index (BMI) is an estimate of a person's body fat. It is calculated by dividing weight (in kilograms) by height (in meters) squared. BMI is used to categorize people into weight categories (underweight, normal, and obese). Yet because muscle weighs more than fat, a very muscular person will have a higher BMI than a person of similar weight and height who is not as physically fit. In spite of its limitations as an indicator of health, measuring average female BMI across the decades reveals several important patterns. The BMI of average women has increased while the BMI of popular fashion icons has decreased. In the 1950s, the difference between these two groups was only four BMI points. Fifty years later, the difference is eleven points. These data show that the "ideal" female form is increasingly unreachable for most women.

Decade	BMI average woman	Ideal woman	BMI ideal woman
1950s	24	Marilyn Monroe	20
1960s	25	Twiggy	15
1980s	25	Cindy Crawford	19
1990s	26	Kate Moss	16
2000s	27	Gisele Bündchen	16

CHAPTER SIX

Big Business and the Bra

The runway sparkles. Lights twinkle. The gathered crowd leans forward. The Angels are coming. This isn't a designer showcase during New York's Fashion Week or the opening number of a hit Broadway musical. This is the annual Victoria's Secret Fashion Show.

The tall, sexy Angels get top billing alongside celebrity performers. Clad only in lingerie, the models work the runway in a riot of music and color, displaying the newest designs from one of the biggest lingerie companies in the world. Victoria's Secret is worth more than $6 billion, and its models are among the most famous—and highest paid—in the fashion industry. Part rock concert and part star-studded party scene, the Victoria's Secret Fashion Show is the culmination of company founder Roy Raymond's vision from back in the 1970s.

THE MALE GAZE

In 1975 feminist film theorist Laura Mulvey wrote an article called "Visual Pleasure and Narrative Cinema." She documented that most Hollywood movies are conceived with male viewers as the target audience. When women are portrayed in movies, their characterization is meant to appeal to heterosexual men. Women most often appear in films as objects of sexual desire. Plot events in the story happen *to* women rather than as a result of their actions. This concept, called "the male gaze," permeates US society and is especially prevalent in advertising. The history of Victoria's Secret is a perfect example of the male gaze in action.

In 1977 thirty-year-old Roy Raymond visited a local California department store, looking for lingerie for his wife. His trip to the store was unsuccessful, not to mention embarrassing and uncomfortable. The store experience was designed for women who were shopping for themselves. What if there was a place that catered to men? Raymond wondered. The store he and his wife opened in Palo Alto, California, that year for $80,000 was inspired by Raymond's fantasy of beautiful women in a nineteenth-century Victorian brothel (a place where sex is exchanged for money), complete with wood paneling, silken curtains, and velvet couches.

Everything about the first Victoria's Secret store catered to the male gaze. It wasn't about women buying functional undergarments. It was about women in lingerie as the object of men's desire.

In 1998 Tyra Banks modeled Victoria's Secret angel wings for the first time in a fashion show. By the early twenty-first century, the Angels models had become so popular they began to tour the world on a regular schedule.

Victoria's Secret was an immediate and huge success. The store raked in $500,000 the first year. By 1982 Raymond and his wife had five stores and a mail-order business that was earning $6 million a year. They sold the company to businessman Les Wexner, and under his leadership, Victoria's Secret continued to grow. Raymond had already proved that appealing to men was good for business. Wexner built on that momentum by convincing female customers that the ideal woman would want to look sexy for her man. Women flocked to Victoria's Secret, wanting to become the sensual object of the male gaze. By 1994 Victoria's Secret was the largest US lingerie company, grossing $1.8 billion each year.

In 1995 Wexner drew on the standard practices of outerwear designers to hold the first Victoria's Secret Fashion Show. It brought underwear into the world of high fashion. In 1998 model Tyra Banks wore the first angel wings on the company's lingerie fashion runway, and thus the Angels were born. In 2000 Wexner introduced another marketing gimmick to the annual fashion show—the fantasy bra. German model Gisele Bündchen showed off the first one, a jewel-encrusted bra worth $15 million. Ever since, a one-of-a-kind, multimillion-dollar bra has been featured at each show. In 2001 the fashion show was aired on television for the first time. By the second decade of the twenty-first century, Victoria's Secret has more than one thousand stores in the United States and is rapidly spreading into Europe and Asia. Annual sales are more than $6.6 billion. Victoria's Secret is bigger, flashier, and fleshier than ever.

THE BRA—AN ENGINEERING MARVEL

In the 1970s, when Victoria's Secret was just getting started, Dorothy Galligan was a cabaret singer who answered a call for a bra-fitting model. Bra models worked for bra designers who painstakingly and with many repetitions created new bras on actual women. Galligan quickly became the most sought-after bra-fitting model in the industry. Galligan's 34Bs were exactly the right size and shape for the fashion of the day. For decades, all the new bras in the United States were created on her body. Larger and smaller sizes were created by proportionally increasing or decreasing bra components.

A Short History of the Wonderbra

In 1939 the Canadian Lady Corset Company licensed the trademark name Wonderbra, but it wasn't until 1960 that the company created a bra with unique uplift features to showcase a woman's breasts. Because the popular look of the time was thin and androgynous, the plunge push-up Wonderbra wasn't a big hit. But by the 1970s, women were trying to show as much cleavage as possible and the popularity of the plunge push-up Wonderbra skyrocketed. Through the decades, the company has featured famous models such as Eva Herzigova. Starring in the company's "Hello Boys" campaign in 1994, she modeled sexy black lingerie on giant billboards. The ads are considered some of the most iconic in advertising history, and Wonderbra continues to be a top-selling brand.

In 2011 billboard advertisers voted Wonderbra's 1994 "Hello Boys" ad as the most iconic in billboard history. The ad, though modest by today's standards, is said to have caused accidents by diverting drivers' attention away from traffic.

The highly engineered structures of the bra are as complex as a suspension bridge. Like the corset before it, a bra must shape and support the breasts and reduce motion. Yet unlike the corset, it must do so without damaging the rib cage, muscles, and soft tissues. Bras must be produced in a huge range of sizes to accommodate both the circumference of the rib cage and the size of the breasts themselves. Measured by weight, breasts range from 0.6 pounds (0.3 kg) to 20 pounds (9 kg). Dave Spector, cofounder with Heidi Zak of the bra company ThirdLove, says, "Most people think of bras as a sexual object [but] it's actually a highly technical garment." The most complex templates have up to forty component parts, from underwires to padding to adjustable straps to clasps. In the design department at

Maidenform, more than fifty people in seven departments are involved in designing a typical bra.

In the twenty-first century, manufacturers rely on more than twenty-six thousand different bra patterns. Some are still based on Galligan's measurements. Women's bodies come in all different shapes and sizes, so it can be a challenge for women to find a bra that fits well and is comfortable. Marks & Spencer, the largest lingerie retailer in the United Kingdom, has six thousand bra fitters on staff. Armed with a measuring tape, these experts fit more than 150,000 customers a month. The key measurements are overbust (torso circumference at nipple level) and underbust (torso circumference underneath the breast). The difference between the two measurements translates to cup size. For example, a 3-inch (7.6 cm) difference between overbust and underbust is a C cup.

But what if your figure doesn't even vaguely resemble Galligan's? That's a problem that Massachusetts Institute of Technology graduate Heidi Zak wants to solve. She plans to revolutionize bra sizing and bra buying. She asked one hundred women of all sizes, shapes, and ages to take digital photos of their breasts with ThirdLove's body-scanning app. It turned out not everyone was a Galligan. "Thirty-seven percent of all women fall between cup sizes," said Zak. ThirdLove offers half sizes and a mobile phone app sizing system so that customers can order from home.

From ThirdLove to Victoria's Secret, lingerie manufacturers of the twenty-first century produce more than six hundred million bras per year. Women wear sports bras, bralettes, push-up bras, and strapless bras in a rainbow of colors and a wide range of fabrics. On average, American women own at least six bras, and this type of garment is a huge part of the $110-billion-dollar global lingerie market.

THE DARK SIDE OF FAST FASHION

Long gone are the days when a woman would care for a hand-sewn corset to ensure that it lasted ten or twenty years. Even farther gone are the days when a fashion trend would last a century.

A High-Tech Bra for Better Health

By the time Julian Rios Cantu (*below*) was thirteen, his mother had survived breast cancer twice, though barely. His childhood in Monterrey, Mexico, had been marked by the intense years she spent battling the disease and recovering from a double mastectomy. He understood that her recovery would have been far easier if doctors had diagnosed her cancer earlier. Why didn't that happen? he wondered. And was there anything he could do about it?

When Cantu was seventeen, he teamed up with three equally high-tech, savvy friends to create a bra that could detect subtle changes in breast health. The result is Eva—the auto-exploration bra. The garment contains two hundred sensors that measure the breast tissue's texture, color, temperature, and blood flow. It's designed to be worn one hour a week. The information collected by Eva is downloaded to a computer that compares the data to that of previous weeks, looking for changes that could indicate the growth of cancer cells.

In 2017 Cantu and his collaborators won the Global Student Entrepreneur Award for their work on Eva. They used the $20,000 prize money to found a start-up company called Higia Technologies to continue their work on early breast cancer diagnosis.

Women near Chennai, India, sew lingerie at an Intimate Fashions factory. Through a partnership with the World Bank, the Pudhu Vaazhvu (New Life) project employs women from rural parts of the region. The women learn skills to earn money that helps them gain independence.

Twenty-first-century designers are churning out new fashion lines every few months. Manufacturers rush the look of the day into production. Retailers get flashy with display and advertising. Consumers try to keep up with changing styles and end up with bursting closets.

US consumers spend more than $250 billion on fashion every year, including $12 billion on lingerie. Altogether, Americans purchase more than 150 billion new pieces of clothing annually. The result is that garments have more in common with single-use plastic water bottles than the clothes of the past, which were often restitched, upgraded, and handed down from mother to daughter or from father to son. Fashion, including undergarments, has become disposable.

The cost of this churning industry is high—not so much in the ten or twenty dollars spent on a bra from a discount retailer but in people and the planet. Fast fashion is a product of globalization, and the garment industry is one of the dirtiest on the planet. The materials themselves often come from petroleum by-products, which are nonrenewable and involve toxic chemicals to produce fabrics. One of these materials is spandex. It is produced by mixing petrochemicals with glycol (an antifreeze), amines (an ammonia-based product), and methyl di-p-phenylene isocyanate (a benzene-based product, which is a petrochemical). Thin, stretchy spandex fibers are woven into most undergarment fabrics of the twenty-first century. Molded plastic clasps, strap adjusters, and the foam pads in breast cups are all petroleum-based products. The metal underwires in modern bras and corsets are made of steel, which requires massive amounts of energy to produce and shape. Even a natural fabric such as cotton is tough on the environment because cotton plants are water guzzlers and farmers spray them with toxic pesticides, which can then run off into nearby waterways. The dyes that color fabrics are often chemical toxins that can pollute local water sources if not disposed of properly. Fabric and clothing factories that use coal and other polluting, nonrenewable, petroleum-based energy sources release vast amounts of carbon dioxide and other greenhouse gases into the atmosphere. The transport of materials and finished garments across the globe by truck and ship—both fueled by petroleum-based products—is also a huge source of carbon pollution. The garment industry alone is responsible for 10 percent of global carbon emissions, making it one of the largest contributors to global warming.

There is also a huge human cost. Once all the component parts for a bra are manufactured, they are shipped to factories to be pieced together. Building a bra is time-consuming and labor-intensive. Very few aspects of construction can be done by automated machines. Most steps in bra assembly are done by factory employees bent over sewing machines. It can take up to three hours to make one bra. The only way that lingerie companies can keep the prices down is by manufacturing items in poor nations where

Mabel Durham Fuller—Union Leader

Historically, most garment workers have been women. In the United States, these women were important members of the labor movement of the early twentieth century. Mabel Durham Fuller was an early leader. In the 1920s, she applied for jobs in garment shops in New York City that hired mostly Jewish and Italian immigrant women. As a black woman, she found it hard to get a job. Once she did, she earned two dollars less per week than her counterparts, even though she was a much better seamstress.

With the support of her coworkers, she fought for equal pay. And in 1922, she was promoted to lead sewing machine operator at the factory where she worked. Under her leadership, Fuller and her coworkers joined the International Ladies' Garment Workers' Union (ILGWU) in 1933. The union worked for equal pay, safe working conditions, and desegregation. To achieve their goals, Fuller and other union women held work strikes (stoppages), picketed discriminatory employers, organized protest marches, put on educational plays, and held fashion shows to raise awareness of workers' rights. In 1941 a group of corset workers in Detroit, Michigan, picketed, wearing only their corsets! Fuller spent her entire life advocating for the rights of women garment workers.

labor costs are low. Much of the work is done by women in China, Bangladesh, India, and Vietnam. The conditions in these factories are far from ideal. For example, women are sometimes locked into poorly ventilated factories and made to work long hours without regular breaks. By one estimate, 98 percent of the women working in clothing and lingerie factories do not earn enough to live on. It's a huge price in human labor for cheap clothes.

Because consumers in the United States and other wealthy nations don't keep clothes for very long, the items we no longer want to wear are piling up around us. Textile waste, including the scraps left over from clothing manufacture and unwanted fashions, is a huge problem according to Tasha Lewis, a professor at Cornell University's Department of Fiber Science and Apparel Design. "We don't necessarily have the ability to handle the disposal," she says. "The rate of disposal is not keeping up with the availability of places

According to Pact Organic's website, organic cotton makes up less than 1 percent of the world's global cotton supply. Yet it requires 71 percent less water and 62 percent less energy than growing conventional cotton does.

to put everything that we're getting rid of and that's the problem." Thrift stores and resale shops offer ways to reuse clothing, but consumers are not so keen to use secondhand bras and underwear because of hygiene concerns.

Some designers are addressing the environmental costs of fast fashion through eco-friendly design. The lingerie company Naja uses fabrics made from recycled plastics and new fabric printing technologies that reduce the water pollution caused by traditional fabric dying. Another company, Pact Organic, uses organic cotton that has been grown with low-water techniques. Only Hearts uses nontoxic dyes. But the only way to really feel good in our skivvies, according to Frances Kozen, associate director of the Cornell Institute of Fashion and Fiber Innovation, is to buy less and keep our clothes longer.

CHAPTER SEVEN

Inside Out

With her songs "Lucky Star," "Like a Virgin," and "Material Girl," pop star and actress Madonna owned the 1980s. Her unconventional sexual style both onstage and offstage infuriated the mainstream and earned her the condemnation of Pope John Paul II, head of the Roman Catholic Church. Yet Madonna's music videos, concerts, and movies were wildly popular, and they brought women's lingerie out of the bedroom and fully into high fashion.

YOU MUST BE MY LUCKY STAR

Capri pants under short skirts.
Black rubber bracelets from wrist to forearm.
Earrings and necklaces with chunky rhinestone-studded crosses.
Torn mesh shirts over black lace bras.

In the 1985 movie *Desperately Seeking Susan,* Madonna plays Susan, a New York City woman who pulls bored suburbanite Roberta, played by Rosanna Arquette, into her bohemian lifestyle. In one scene, Madonna wears a white garter belt and lace stockings over a pair of shorts. In another, she sports a black lace crop top

Madonna rocketed to stardom in the mid-1980s with the film *Desperately Seeking Susan* and her first concert tour (the Virgin Tour). Underwear as outerwear was her signature look in stage concerts such as this one in 1985.

that clearly shows off the bra underneath. Because of Madonna, exposed bras, corsets, garters, and stockings became key elements of a new look.

Madonna wore lingerie in her stage shows too. Her clothes and her sexually charged performances brought female sexuality and rebellion out into the open. She wasn't hinting at sexuality or being subtly subversive. Instead, Madonna yelled her rejection of feminine social norms.

For the Blond Ambition World Tour in 1990, Madonna wore a pale pink, one-piece belted corset with a front zipper from crotch to cleavage and a pink garter belt with black stockings. The corset's exaggerated breast cups were large and conical, with in-your-face protruding points. French high-fashion designer Jean Paul Gaultier, who designed the outfit, was inspired by the bullet bras of the 1950s. The garment connects historically confining lingerie with modern eroticism and female power by merging soft pastel pink with aggressive lines.

Madonna's 1990 "Vogue" music video evokes the Hollywood glamour and style of the past through images and lyrics that recall stars such as Marilyn Monroe, Jean Harlow, Greta Garbo, Ginger Rogers, Rita Hayworth, and Bette Davis.

In the video, Madonna makes many costume changes, including a see-through camisole, an exaggerated velvet cone bra, and a re-creation of the Mainbocher corset made famous by photographer Horst P. Horst in the 1930s.

"Vogue" was not only about fashion and lingerie. It also challenged gender and sexual identity norms, featuring acrobatic voguing, a dance form that emulates model-like poses from fashion magazines. Voguing originated in the 1960s in the gay nightclub scene of New York's Harlem neighborhood, particularly among black and Latino drag performers. Madonna hired some of these gender-bending dancers for her video, which brought mainstream attention to the dance style. Madonna's video was openly admiring of lesbian, gay, bisexual, transgender, queer or questioning (LGBTQ) style, which made its way into haute couture (high fashion).

HAUTE COUTURE

Gaultier isn't the only designer to use lingerie front and center in high fashion collections. Corsets have inspired the work of John Galliano, Karl Lagerfeld,

Fetish Wear

Fetishism is a form of erotic, or sexual, play that focuses on specific objects or pieces of clothing. The term arose in the late nineteenth century from *feitiço*, a Portuguese word that refers to an obsessive fascination. A person with a fetish experiences sexual excitement from an object of fascination—high-heeled boots or corsets, for example.

Jean Paul Gaultier, the French designer who made Madonna's famous cone bra, said, "The first fetish I did was a corset. That was because of my grandmother." When he found one of her corsets in a closet and asked about it, his grandmother told him about the tight lacing of the Victorian era. He was captivated by the secret history of the garment. Like Victorian fetishists, some gay and straight men wear corsets for fantasy play. Fetish wear is a way that some people use to push back against traditional gender roles.

Models such as Bettie Page from the 1950s and pop stars such as Madonna in the 1990s have used corsets to express female power and sexuality. By doing so, they too are challenging gender roles.

Beyoncé and high-fashion designer Thierry Mugler have collaborated on many of the megastar's stage shows. Mugler says he designs her costumes, many of which use lingerie as the foundational garments, to be "Feminine. Free. Warrior. Fierce."

Tom Ford, Gianni Versace, Valentino, Vivienne Westwood, Issey Miyake, Hussein Chalayan, Alexander McQueen, Christian Lacroix, and Thierry Mugler. These designers use visible corsetry to express a wide range of ideas about women, femininity, power, sexuality, and gender identity.

Corset-inspired creations by French fashion designer Thierry Mugler, for example, are far more than just garments. His works combine soft fabrics with hard materials such as leather, Plexiglas, and metal to encase the female body. When wearing these corsets, a model is transformed into a mythic Amazon, an armored knight, a biker, a robot, an alien, or an insect. Mugler's fierce fashions evoke strong reactions. Some are offended by his fetish-inspired designs. Some are shocked by garments that seem almost like an act of violence against the model's body. Others see his work as transformative, elevating the female form to something more than human.

In 2008 pop sensation Beyoncé attended an event at the Costume Institute Gala at the Metropolitan Museum in New York called *Superheroes: Fashion and Fantasy.* The exhibition paired actual costumes from superhero movies with pieces by famous designers. One of Mugler's corset designs, which drew on motorcycle parts, transformed a model into part-vehicle, part-human. Beyoncé was so impressed that she commissioned Mugler to design costumes for her United Kingdom tour. She also chose a powerful, sexy photograph of herself wearing a Mugler motorcycle corset for the liner notes of her 2008 album *I Am . . . Sasha Fierce.*

QUEEN BEY

On February 1, 2017, long after the motorcycle corset, Beyoncé posted a photo to Instagram to announce that she and husband, Jay Z, were expecting twins. In the photo, taken by Ethiopian American multimedia artist Awol Erizku, Beyoncé kneels against a profusion of flowers, with her hands on her pregnant belly. She is radiant, wearing only a pair of ruffled, blue silk underpants, a sheer maroon bra, and a pale green veil.

Scholars and fans immediately began to analyze the image. Artistically, Beyoncé's portrait recalls the lush, colorful paintings of Frida Kahlo and Gustav Klimt. It also brings to mind the works of modern artists such as Kehinde Wiley and Mickalene Thomas, who feature people of color against bright, floral backgrounds. The intensely vivid colors of Beyoncé's lingerie and the blissfully happy look on her face reminded many of the colorful Our Lady of Guadalupe (a Roman Catholic image of the Virgin Mary) in Mexico City.

In the photograph, Beyoncé stares right at the camera. Katie Edwards, the director of the Sheffield Institute for Interdisciplinary Biblical Studies in the United Kingdom, says Beyoncé's look is an example of "the oppositional gaze." Cultural critic bell hooks (who does not capitalize her name) coined this term in the early 1990s. Like the male gaze, the oppositional gaze is an idea from film theory. The male gaze, hooks says, is based on the notion of white women as the objects of sexual desire for heterosexual men. For black Americans, the gaze is more complex. Black Americans have historically faced severe punishment, even murder, for looking directly at white people. Looking is, therefore, a political act for people of color, hooks points out. She says, "All attempts to repress our/black peoples' right to gaze had produced in us an overwhelming longing to look, a rebellious desire, an oppositional gaze."

In Erizku's photograph, Beyoncé offers her own oppositional gaze. She confronts racist stereotypes of women of color as sexually aggressive, primitive, and exotic. According to Edwards, this message is communicated specifically by Beyoncé's choice to pair lingerie with religious imagery such as her veil (which is associated with the Virgin Mary) and kneeling posture. In the portrait—the most popular Instagram post of all time with more than eleven million likes—Beyoncé claims her sensuality, her personal power, and her maternal side. She is Queen Bey.

PROTEST AND THE SHATTERED BODY

Beyoncé is not the only artist to use lingerie to make a statement about society and the female body. Since the 1960s, feminist artists have depicted

Barbara Kruger made the "Your Body Is a Battleground" poster (*left*) in 1991 to protest a series of court decisions that were chipping away at the constitutional right to abortion. Artist activists use artwork to protest other restrictions on women's bodies, including undergarments.

undergarments in photographs, sculptures, paintings, and mixed media work. These pieces focus on the experiences of the female body—menstruation, sex, pregnancy, childbirth, assault, athleticism, aging, pleasure, and pain.

Laura Jacobs sculpts three-dimensional female torsos. Each one is wearing undergarments—bras and panties, traditional corsets, or erotic fetish wear—made of shattered glass, tile, or shell. Each mosaic piece has an evocative, punning title such as *Fertile Crescents* or *The Breast of Both Whorls.* Jacobs's website says of her work, "No longer bound by constraints of clothing alone, women may now have the delightful pleasure of deforming themselves from the inside out."

Nancy Davidson uses giant latex balloons to create voluptuous hanging sculptures of breasts (that also double as eyes) in lacy bras. She also creates bulbous butt cheeks wearing frilly G-strings. One piece called *Blue Moon* is a huge blue balloon laced into a giant, white corset. The balloon bulges out at the top and bottom of the corset. About her own work, Davidson

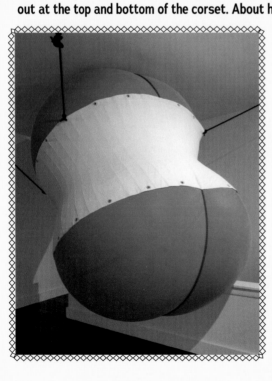

says, "You laugh at the enormous breasts, the big butt, and suddenly it's like, 'Oh my God, what am I laughing at, why is this sexual thing making me so uncomfortable?'"

Nancy Davidson uses latex, rope, and cotton to create her inflatable body sculptures. Her in-your-face-humor is meant to nudge viewers to think about the ways fashion forces bodies into random, often absurd shapes. This sculpture, called *Blue Moon*, features a body squeezing out of a giant, white corset.

Miriam Schaer's work was inspired by medieval girdle books—prayer books that monks tied to their girdles (belts). She takes corsets and stiffens them until they are solid and unbending. She slits them open and then uses the two halves of the garment as the cover of a book. The book holds images and small items such as feathers or a multilayered Jewish Star of David. Schaer says, "The garment becomes immobile, as if the wearer evaporated, leaving only a shell. They [the corsets] become places. Enclosures. Upon opening, the ghost of the missing person still remains in the echo of the garment's fixed shape."

Musicians such as Madonna and Beyoncé and visual artists such as Jacobs, Davidson, and Schaer use women's undergarments as social commentary. For them, a woman's body has always been a battlefield.

CHAPTER EIGHT

The Perfect Body

In 2014 Victoria's Secret ramped up an advertising campaign to launch a new line of bras and underwear called Body. The print campaign featured ten lingerie-clad Angels in a lineup. The campaign slogan—THE PERFECT "BODY"—was emblazoned over their supermodel curves.

Women around the world responded with outrage. Thirty-three thousand women signed a Change.org petition called #IAmPerfect. They asked for the company to recall the campaign and to apologize for promoting unhealthy and unrealistic beauty standards for women. Journalist Sarah Vine criticized the Victoria's Secret campaign saying, "As for their use of the word 'perfect', it's not only offensive to the 99.9% of the female population who don't share the models' 'perfect' proportions, it's also deeply irresponsible, if not downright cruel."

Dear Kate, an underwear company, published its own ad in response, featuring normal-sized women in tank tops and underwear. In another response, ten British women of all ages and body types re-created the Victoria's Secret ad, wearing the same lingerie and posing in the same positions as the professional models. Each participant shared why she had chosen to be so exposed. Gail Daniel from Leicestershire, England, said, "I'm fed up of ads making women feel bad about ourselves. Why can't we stop beating ourselves up about our bodies?" Suzanne

Dalmedo from Berkshire, added, "I want to show my little girl that women should love their bodies." Thirty-four-year-old Natalie Lee from East London said, "The fashion industry needs to realise women come in every size—and we are all perfect."

Many women experience lingerie ads like the Perfect Body campaign as a form of body shaming. Body shaming can take many forms: equating "pretty" with only one body shape in television, movies, books, and online; assuming that anyone who doesn't have a supermodel body is stupid, lazy, or unworthy of love; making jokes about a person's body or clothing; or criticizing someone's food or exercise choices. Body shaming can damage a person's self-esteem and be a contributing factor in eating disorders such as anorexia and bulimia.

Gail Daniel, Suzanne Dalmedo, Natalie Lee, and the other real-life women who decided to be photographed in lingerie were rebelling against a restrictive definition of beauty. The protest said to the world, "I am perfect."

Underwear company Dear Kate created a body-positive ad, representing all types of female-identified bodies in their underwear. The ad was a response to the Victoria's Secret Perfect "Body" campaign, which offended women around the world.

Zendaya Claps Back

Model, actor, musician, fashion designer, and young feminist Zendaya has dealt with her share of body shaming. After a 2016 appearance on Nickelodeon's Kids' Choice Awards, Zendaya got trolled on Twitter for being too skinny. Both she and her fans clapped back:

@Zendaya: "Do you find this funny?"

@brokeymcpoverty: "Time to stop using women's bodies for laughs, whether fat or skinny."

@Zendaya: "Now . . . everyone go look in the mirror at their beautiful body, and love that s#%$ #thickgirlswinning #skinnygirlswinning #weallwinning

Then in 2017, Zendaya stumbled on a Twitter troll bullying a young woman online. She roared her outrage:

@Zendaya: "She is fine as hell head to toe and garunteed [sic] doesn't know you exist my man. As for her, slay on queen."

And followed up with a call for her fans to help track down the young woman:

@Zendaya: "I'd love for her to be a @dayabyzendaya model."

It didn't take long! The young woman's response is pretty priceless:

@_illestCee: "im really speechless right now because becoming a plus size model has been my number one goal"

IN THE PRINCIPAL'S OFFICE

Damaging messages about body image directed at women are nothing new. There has always been intense pressure on women to meet the ideal. Increasingly the "right" shape for women is highly sexualized. The media presents images of women in sexy underwear to sell everything from trucks to perfume. The message to women couldn't be clearer: this is what you should look like if you want men to want you. But women are also bombarded with the exact opposite message. Don't be too sexy or wear something too revealing because if you do, men won't be able to control their sexual urges. You'll be called a slut or worse.

Men are sexualized in the media too, but not to the same extent. They do not face the same restrictions and expectations of what is acceptable to wear. This double standard—having one set of rules for women and different rules for men—is especially obvious in the debate about school dress codes, which often target girls. School rules might forbid leggings, shorts, miniskirts, tank tops, exposed bra straps, visible shoulders, sheer blouses, or anything else deemed too provocative. Schools often enforce the codes unevenly. Girls are called out for dress code violations far more often than boys. Heavier girls are called out more often than thin ones. Gender nonconforming teens often run afoul of school dress codes too. Aniya Wolf from Bishop McDevitt High School in Pennsylvania was sent home from her prom in 2016 for wearing a tuxedo instead of a gown. Her school refused to budge, but Aniya and her girlfriend were invited and went to prom at nearby William Penn High School instead.

When school dress codes focus on boys, the restrictions are almost always on clothing that is considered disrespectful or gang-related. This can include T-shirts with provocative words or images. Most often, however, disrespectful clothing usually refers to sagging—a fashion trend that originated among young black males in the late 1980s. It is associated with rap and hip-hop culture. The pants are worn low on the hips so that the top half of the underwear is exposed. School administrators sometimes call the look urban or ghetto. Both terms have deeply racist implications that wrongly associate black men with criminality.

GROWING UP TOO FAST

More and more very young girls are having to deal with increasing sexualization of dress. In 2002, for example, Abercrombie & Fitch released a line of thong underwear, sized for elementary-aged girls, with *eye candy* and *wink* printed on the front of the thongs. In 2011 the same company sold a skimpy bikini swimsuit for girls as young as seven. The padded cups of the top piece of the suit gave the child the appearance of having fully developed breasts. And then there's bum writing. From underwear to sweatpants to leggings, tween-focused companies sell tight clothes with brand logos—Pink or Juicy—printed across the backside of the garment.

A Bratz doll known as Cloe is just one of many highly sexualized dolls for young girls. A bustier, short flouncy skirt, and superhigh ankle boots are part of the look.

And it's not just clothes that spread the message that girl children are sex objects. Dolls for little girls come with sexualized clothes and undergarments such as fishnet stockings, corsets, and lacy dance hall skirts. Youth beauty pageants feature young girls in heavy makeup doing sexual dance moves, wearing skimpy swimsuits, and imitating sex symbols such as Madonna and Marilyn Monroe.

Social psychologist Sarah K. Murnen from Kenyon College in Ohio and several of her students analyzed sexualized images of girls in teen magazines. They looked at thousands of advertisements and tallied characteristics such as low-cut shirts, bare midriffs, visible lingerie, high heels, and other adult features. From 1971 to 2011, the number of sexualized images in *Seventeen* magazine tripled, and the number of sexualized images that appeared in *Girl's Life* in 2011 was fifteen times greater than in 1994.

In a 2007 report from the American Psychological Association's Task Force on the Sexualization of Girls, researchers identified four characteristics that separate damaging sexualization from healthy sexuality:

1. A girl's value is related to her sexiness.
2. Her attractiveness depends on how sexy she is.
3. She is an object for the sexual pleasure of men.
4. Her level of sexual expression is imposed by others.

The report concluded that sexualization of girls negatively affects their self-esteem, often leads to depression, and plays a key role in the development of eating disorders. Lead researcher Eileen Zurbriggen from the University of California at Santa Cruz said, "The consequences of the sexualization of girls in media today are very real. . . . We have ample evidence to conclude that sexualization has negative effects in a variety of domains, including cognitive [brain or thought] functioning, physical and mental health, and healthy sexual development."

FROM FRUSTRATED CONSUMERS TO CEOs

Lingerie is a multibillion-dollar industry that is run primarily by men. Men design the undergarments, market them, plan the fashion shows, and run lingerie companies. They profit from the low-wage labor of women working in substandard conditions. They also profit from purchases that women and girls make to try to meet the standards imposed on women through media images. But twenty-first-century female entrepreneurs are changing the garment industry from the inside out. Out of frustration with sexist ideas of what women should or shouldn't look like and what they should or shouldn't wear, women are starting companies that do things differently.

Megan Grassell, founder of Yellowberry, designs comfortable, age-appropriate underwear for tweens. The company's site offers information about body positivity, buying tips for first bras, and more. You can even join Megan's Book Club and read books about strong girls.

Megan Grassell was seventeen years old when she took her younger sister bra shopping at the mall. It was a disaster! Nothing fit right. Every bra was padded, cleavage enhancing, and way too sexy. Grassell kept wondering, "Why wasn't there just a cute, colorful and

Gina Rodriguez is a cofounder of Naja. The company believes in supporting the workers who make Naja garments. They do this, not just with salaries, but by providing each worker's children with books, school supplies, and school uniforms. Naja also pays for school meals.

comfortable bra for Mary Margaret to fit her and her body, not the body that she was "supposed" to have? The answer was that there simply wasn't one." Grassell thought tweens should have age-appropriate bras, and she decided to take matters into her own hands. In 2014, when she was a junior in high school, Grassell founded Yellowberry, a bra company for tweens. Her company offers cute bras in bright colors that provide support but don't artificially enhance cleavage. Every detail is designed for tween comfort, not sex appeal. The company's packaging and advertising offer messages of girl power. In 2014 Grassell was selected by *Time* magazine as one of the 25 Most Influential Teens of the Year, and Yellowberry continues to grow.

Another female entrepreneur tired of sexism in the lingerie industry is Colombian-born entrepreneur Catalina Girald. Frustrated with the Victoria's Secret focus on men and what men find sexy, she and *Jane the Virgin* star Gina Rodriguez founded San Francisco-based Naja (pronounced nah-yah), a company focused on women. Girald says their mission is "delivering luxury lingerie at fair prices while empowering women." Girald's designs focus on the woman wearing the lingerie rather than on the male gaze. Every bra is lined with colorful fabric so that it is as beautiful on the inside as on the outside. Each pair of underwear has an inspirational quote—*Be Your Own Kind of Beautiful* or *Don't Be Afraid to Ask for What You Want*—printed on the inside of the crotch for only the wearer to see. Girard is committed to her female employees as well. She says, "If we were going to empower women who wore

[Naja], we needed to empower the women who made them too." She works with a nonprofit organization in her hometown of Medellín, Colombia, in a project called Underwear for Hope. This program teaches poor and single mothers to sew and gives them jobs sewing for Naja with fair wages and flexible schedules so they can take care of their children.

British businesswoman Ade Hassan's complaint with the lingerie industry was that it focused on white women to the exclusion of women of color. Nude, one of the industry's top-selling underwear colors, is a pale pink intended to be worn under light-colored and sheer blouses. But when Hassan, whose skin tone is dark brown, wore a typical nude bra under a white shirt, the bra stood out instead of blending in. She launched her company, Nubian Skin, in 2014. It sells bras and panties in four nude skin tones, ranging from dark brown to tan. Her ad campaigns feature brown-skinned women celebrating high-fashion lingerie in nudes that work for them.

Hayat Rachi, another activist-innovator from the United Kingdom, is the daughter of Moroccan immigrants. She remembers being bullied as a kid.

Neon Moon CEO & Founder, Hayat:

"I want to use my past experiences and passion for body-positivity to create a better world for women, with women. I want women to be comfortable, inspired and to empower each other."

Hayat Rachi founded Neon Moon in 2015. Her underwear company is committed to body positivity. To achieve this, the company does not edit out body hair, cellulite, or rolls of skin in photographs of models. The company believes that all bodies are beautiful.

Uniting Body and Mind

Historically, undergarments have been markers of gender. Tighty-whities or satin thongs? Bras or undershirts? Pantyhose or gym socks? But what if you are experiencing gender dysphoria, in which your sense of gender identity (masculine or feminine or neither) doesn't match your biological gender (male, female, or intersex)? Finding great undergarments that work with your gender identity can help you feel way more comfortable in your own skin.

Innovative lingerie designers want to help. Cy Lauz, for example, founded Chrysalis Lingerie in 2013 to design and sell lingerie for transgender women. Not all trans women have gender-confirming surgery to match their genitals with their gender. So Lauz's underwear has an inner panel to tuck and hold the penis between the legs and mesh panels to reduce bulges. Chrysalis Lingerie also sells padded, bust-enhancing bras. For trans men, not all of whom have surgery to remove their breasts, Laura Treas at All Is Fair in Love and Wear offers chest binders and other garments that create a flatter, male body shape on top. Origami Customs sells a brief designed to hold a stand-to-pee device so that trans men with vaginas not penises can use urinals. All of these garments are available online.

Besides having functional undergarments, trans people also want beautiful things to wear under their clothes. As trans man Teddy Tinnell says, "The parts of our bodies that are the most dysphoric need the most tenderness and love."

"When I was in school, people would point out my appearance and laugh [about my] curly Moroccan hair, big nose, small breasts and body hair!" Rachi founded Neon Moon in 2015 to make body-positive lingerie and spread a message of body acceptance. The Neon Moon website and its ads feature real women of all sizes, shapes, and ethnicities—complete with stretch marks, blemishes, freckles, tattoos, and body hair. Selfies on the website offer a wide variety of images of women in Neon Moon undergarments, which are all made in the United Kingdom. The site even introduces the women who make the underwear!

"Girls," says Rachi, "should not have to question why they look a certain way. . . . Rather they need to reclaim the right to their bodies and decide how it should look for them and not for others."

EXPRESS YOURSELF

In November 2016, nineteen-year-old Halima Aden competed in the Miss Minnesota USA pageant. For each event, she took the stage wearing a hijab, a headscarf worn by some Muslim women that covers the head and neck. During the swimsuit portion of the pageant, she wore a burkini, a swimming garment that covers most of a woman's body. When asked about her choice of attire, Aden said, "I just want to go on as myself. When you have a lot of women in our state that do wear the hijab, we should be able to see that everywhere." For Aden, this was about choice.

In many parts of the world, such as the United States and Turkey (a secular, nonreligious, Muslim-majority nation), Muslim women have the choice of whether

Somali American model Halima Aden wears a burkini in the first bathing suit round of the Miss Minnesota USA pageant in November 2016. Aden has gone on to become an internationally famous fashion model.

to wear a headscarf. But in other parts of the world, such as Saudi Arabia and Iran (Muslim-majority nations that follow strict religious guidelines), women are required by law to wear a concealing garment. These garments may be a hijab, a burqa (a one-piece veil that covers the head, neck, face, and the rest of the body), or a niqab (a veil that covers the lower half of the face and is worn with a headscarf). Other secular, predominantly Christian countries, such as France, Switzerland, and the Netherlands, have large populations of Muslims. These nations have chosen to ban concealing garments as well as modest burkini swimwear in public. In one case, armed police officers on a beach in France tried to force a woman to remove her burkini.

The global controversies over traditional Muslim garb reflect the complex issues about women and appearance in modern life. Who decides what women can wear? Do secular nations have the right to impose values that impact how women from modest cultures dress? Is it a religious issue? Is it a race issue? Is it a feminist issue? Americans live in a society that values youth, beauty, and sex appeal, but feminism isn't just about appearances. It's about creating opportunities for all women to be in charge of their own lives.

When Aden's mother, a refugee from Somalia, was asked about her daughter's participation in a beauty pageant, she said, "This is something new to me. I'm very happy to live in the United States where people are free and can wear what they want." Perhaps the modern era represents a fundamental change in the history of women's underwear. Instead of controlling women, intimate apparel can be a form of self-expression and self-adoration. Whether she chooses cotton or lace, what matters most is the woman wearing the lingerie and what she wants to say about herself.

SOURCE NOTES

5   "Girl Undresses in Public for Courageous Cause," YouTube video, 1:29, posted by Liberators International, August 14, 2015, https://youtu.be/AJFrHwBtfJw.

6   Jae West, "The Story of the Girl Undressing in Public," *Inspiralight* (blog), August 15, 2015, http://inspiralight. wordpress.com/2015/08/15/the-story-of-the-girl-undressing-in-public-written-by-jae-west/.

6   "Girl Undresses," YouTube.

6   Ibid.

7   Ibid.

7   Carly Stern, "Mother-of Three Strips Down to a Bikini in the Middle of a Busy Market While Blindfolded and Invites Strangers to Draw Hearts on Her Body in an Effort to Promote Self-Love," *Daily Mail* (London), September 9, 2015, http://www.dailymail.co.uk/femail/article-3228045/Mother-three-strips-bikini-middle-busy -marketplace-invites-strangers-draw-hearts-body-effort-promote-self-love.html.

7   West, "The Story of the Girl Undressing."

13   Henri de Mondeville, quoted in Charlotte Hodgman, "Medieval Underwear," *History Extra*, November 17, 2015, http://www.historyextra.com/lingerie.

14   Hope Bridges Adams Lehmann, quoted in Lecia Bushak, "A Brief History of the Menstrual Period: How Women Dealt with Their Cycles throughout the Ages," *Medical Daily*, May 23, 2016, http://www.medicaldaily.com /menstrual-period-time-month-history-387252.

27   Unidentified journalist, quoted in Valerie Steele, *The Corset: A Cultural History* (New Haven, CT: Yale University Press, 2001), 27.

28   Ibid., 12.

28   Ibid.

34   Quoted in Jill Fields, *An Intimate Affair: Women, Lingerie, and Sexuality* (Berkeley: University of California Press, 2007), 28.

34   Amelia Bloomer, quoted in Norma Shephard. *Lingerie: Two Centuries of Luscious Design* (Atglen, PA: Schiffer, 2008), 9.

35   New York Times editorial board, quoted in Fields, *An Intimate Affair: Women,* . . . (. . .), 26.

37   Author unknown, quoted in Chelsea Summers, "The Politics of Pockets," *Racked*, September 19, 2016, http:// www.racked.com/2016/9/19/12865560/politics-of-pockets-suffragettes-women.

37   Christian Dior, quoted in Chelsea Summers, "The Politics of Pockets," *Racked*, September 19, 2016, http://www. racked.com/2016/9/19/12865560/politics-of-pockets-suffragettes-women.

39   Author unknown, quoted in Hollis Clayson, *Painted Love: Prostitution in French Art of the Impressionist Era* (Los Angeles: Getty Research Institute, 2003), 75.

39   Ibid.

40 Gustav Jaeger, quoted in Valerie Steele, *The Corset: A Cultural History* (New Haven, CT: Yale University Press, 2001), 80–81.

41 Luke Limner, quoted in Valerie Steele, *The Corset: A Cultural History* (New Haven, CT: Yale University Press, 2001), 67.

46 Caresse Crosby, quoted in Michael Ruane, "Caresse Crosby, Who Claimed the Invention of the Bra, Was Better Known for Her Wild Life," *Washington Post,* November 11, 2014, https://www.washingtonpost.com/local/caresse -crosby-who-claimed-the-invention-of-the-bra-was-better-known-for-her-wild-life/2014/11/09/99c55f7e-3f39 -11e4-b03f-de718edeb92f_story.html.

46 Ibid.

46 Caresse Crosby, quoted in Jill Fields, *An Intimate Affair: Women, Lingerie, and Sexuality* (Berkeley: University of California Press, 2007), 82.

49 Eliza Berman, "This Is What the Ideal Woman Looked Like in the 1930s," *Time,* June 2, 2015, http://time .com/3860561/ideal-woman-1930s/.

53 Liz Welch, "Face It: Your Bra Sucks," *Inc.,* accessed December 17, 2016, http://www.inc.com/magazine/201611 /liz-welch/busting-out-feminine-product-revolution.html.

61 Ibid.

62 Ibid.

67 Zhai Yun Tan, "What Happens When Fashion Becomes Fast, Disposable and Cheap?," *NPR,* April 10, 2016, http:// www.npr.org/2016/04/08/473513620/what-happens-when-fashion-becomes-fast-disposable-and-cheap.

70 Jean Paul Gaultier, quoted in Valerie Steele, *The Corset: A Cultural History* (New Haven, CT: Yale University Press, 2001), 168.

71 Tracey Lomrantz Leste, "Beyonce's "I Am . . . " World Tour Costumes Are Redefining Fierce," *Glamour.com,* March 26, 2009, https://www.glamour.com/story/beyonces-i-am-world-tour-costu.

73 bell hooks, "The Oppositional Gaze: Black Female Spectators," in *Black Looks: Race and Representation* (Boston: South End, 1992), 115–131.

74 "Foundation Art." Laura Ann Jacobs, accessed May 30, 2017, http://www.lauraannjacobs.com/foundation.php.

74 "The Titillating Balloon Art of Nancy Davidson," *Jeremyriad,* November 21, 2012, http://www.jeremyriad.com/ blog/art/sculptures/the-titillating-balloon-art-of-nancy-davidson.

75 "Girdle Books," Miriam Schaer, accessed May 30, 2017, http://www.miriamschaer.com/girdle-books.

76 Hayley Peterson, "Victoria's Secret Sparks Outrage with 'Perfect Body' Campaign," *Business Insider,* October 31, 2014, http://www.businessinsider.com/victorias-secret-perfect-body-campaign-2014-10.

76 Jill Foster, "We're Perfectly Normal!," *Daily Mail* (London), November 7, 2014, http://www.dailymail.co.uk/femail /article-2826017/We-perfectly-normal-Victoria-s-Secret-s-new-ad-attacked-calling-waif-like-models-perfect -look-like-real-women-talk-frankly-bodies.html.

77 Ibid.

77 Ibid.

78 Zendaya, Twitter post, 7:46 a.m., March 13, 2016, https://twitter.com/Zendaya/status /709027742293970944.

78 Tracy Clayton, Twitter post, 2:14 p.m., March 13, 2016, https://twitter.com/brokeymcpoverty/status /709125404494340097.

78 Zendaya, Twitter post, 7:52 a.m., March 13, 2016, https://twitter.com/Zendaya/status /709029343805050880.

78 Zendaya, Twitter post, 5:48 p.m., January 27, 2017, https://twitter.com/Zendaya/status /825158523902423041.

78 Zendaya, Twitter post, 5:48 p.m., January 27, 2017, https://twitter.com/Zendaya/status/825158651451146241.

78 Honey Dip, Twitter post, 6:00 p.m., January 27, 2017, https://twitter.com/_illestCee/status /825161548645687296.

81 Krysta Jones and Corine Bell, "Protecting Girls: APA Continues to Lead Advocacy Efforts against Sexualization," *Monitor on Psychology*, July/August 2011, http://www.apa.org/monitor/2011/07-08/protecting-girls.aspx.

82 Beth Greenfield, "Mom Outraged a Training Bra Claims to 'Smooth Imperfections,'" *Yahoo Style*, September 6, 2016, https://www.yahoo.com/style/mom-outraged-a-training-bra-claims-to-smooth -imperfections-153844402.html.

82 Erika Brown Ekiel, "Catalina Girald: 'I Want to Change Women's Lives,'" Stanford Graduate School of Business, April 17, 2014, https://www.gsb.stanford.edu/insights/catalina-girald-i-want-change-womens-lives.

83 Barbara Gonzalez, "Creating Espacios: Catalina Girald Talks Building a Brand Based on Empowerment," *Forbes*, August 9, 2016, http://www.forbes.com/sites/barbaragonzalez/2016/08/09/catalina-girald-talks-building-a -brand-based-on-empowerment.

84 "About Us," Neon Moon, accessed October 19, 2015, https://www.neonmoon.co/pages/about-us.

84 "'You Are Not Just a Body': The Feminist Mantra of Neon Moon," *Lingerie Talk,* March 13, 2015, http://www .lingerietalk.com/2015/03/13/lingerie-news/you-are-not-just-a-body-the-feminist-mantra-of-neon-moon.html.

84 Angelina Chapin, "Underwear for Trans People: The Torture of Binding, Tucking and Packing Is Over," *Guardian* (US ed.), September 24, 2015, https://www.theguardian.com/lifeandstyle/2015/sep/24/underwear-for -transgender-people-shapewear.

85 Ashley Collman, "Somali-American Teen Becomes the First Miss USA Hopeful to Wear a Hijab and a Burkini," *Daily Mail* (London), November 28, 2016, http://www.dailymail.co.uk/news/article-3978174/Muslim-woman -wears-hijab-burkini-Minnesota-pageant.html.

86 Ibid.

SELECTED BIBLIOGRAPHY

Barbier, Muriel, and Shazia Boucher. *The Story of Women's Underwear*. New York: Parkstone, 2010.

Benson, Elaine, and John Esten. *Unmentionables: A Brief History of Underwear*. New York: Simon & Schuster, 1996.

Carter, Alison. *Underwear: The Fashion History*. New York: Drama, 1992.

Cole, Shaun. *The Story of Men's Underwear*. New York: Parkstone, 2010.

Cunnington, C. Willett. *The History of Underclothes*. Mineola, NY: Dover, 1992.

Ewing, Elizabeth. *Dress & Undress*. London: B. T. Batsford, 1978.

Fields, Jill. *An Intimate Affair: Women, Lingerie, and Sexuality*. Berkeley: University of California Press, 2007.

Fitch, Anna. *Man Made: Secret History of the Bra*. First broadcast on the National Geographic channel, October 5, 2007.

Hill, Colleen. *Exposed: A History of Lingerie*. New Haven, CT: Yale University Press, 2014.

Shephard, Norma. *Lingerie: Two Centuries of Luscious Design*. Atglen, PA: Schiffer, 2008.

Steele, Valerie. *The Corset: A Cultural History*. New Haven, CT: Yale University Press, 2001.

FURTHER INFORMATION

Books

Cline, Elizabeth. *Overdressed: The Shockingly High Cost of Cheap Fashion.* New York: Portfolio, 2013.

Donovan, Sandy. *Thrift Shopping: Discovering Bargains and Hidden Treasures.* Minneapolis: Twenty-First Century Books, 2015.

Higgins, Nadia Abushanab. *Feminism: Reinventing the F-word.* Minneapolis: Twenty-First Century Books, 2016.

O'Neill, Terese. *Unmentionable: The Victorian Lady's Guide to Sex, Marriage, and Manners.* New York: Little, Brown, 2016.

Rutledge, Jill S. Zimmerman. *Prom: The Big Night Out.* Minneapolis: Twenty-First Century Books, 2017.

Stein, Elissa, and Susan Kim. *Flow: The Cultural Story of Menstruation.* New York: St. Martin's Griffin, 2009.

Tobin, Shelly. *Inside Out: A Brief History of Underwear.* London: National Trust, 2000.

Films

"Girl Undresses in Public for Courageous Cause." YouTube video, 1:29. Posted by Liberators International, August 14, 2015. This is the story of Jae West undressing in Picadilly Circus to raise awareness about self-esteem and body positivity.

Revealing Garments: A Brief History of Women's Underwear. YouTube video, 1:04:56. Posted by the Indianapolis Museum of Art, November 15, 2012. https://youtube/AJ6eqMgn5u0. H. Kristina Haugland, the associate curator of Costume and Textiles at the Philadelphia Museum of Art, discusses the history of women's underwear.

"Women's Ideal Body Types throughout History." YouTube video, 3:09. Posted by BuzzFeedVideo, January 26, 2015. https://youtube/XrpOzJZuOa4. The changing standards of female beauty for the last three thousand years are the focus of this video.

Online Articles

Bédat, Maxine, and Michael Shank. "There Is a Major Climate Issue Hiding in Your Closet: Fast Fashion." *Fast Company,* November 11, 2016. https://www.fastcoexist.com/3065532/there-is-a-major-climate-issue-hiding-in-your -closet-fast-fashion.

Chapin, Angelina. "Underwear for Trans People: The Torture of Binding, Tucking and Packing Is Over." *Guardian* (US ed.), September 24, 2015. https://www.theguardian.com/lifeandstyle/2015/sep/24/underwear-for-transgender -people-shapewear.

Chase, Loretta, and Susan Holloway. "More about Corsets: Baleen Ho!" *Two Nerdy History Girls* (blog), April 7, 2010. http://twonerdyhistorygirls.blogspot.com/2010/04/more-about-corsets-baleen-ho.html.

Edwards, Katie. "How Beyoncé Pregnancy Pics Challenge Racist, Religious and Sexual Stereotypes." *Conversation,* February 5, 2017. http://theconversation.com/how-beyonce-pregnancy-pics-challenge-racist-religious-and- sexual-stereotypes-72429.

hooks, bell. "The Oppositional Gaze: Black Female Spectators." In *Black Looks: Race and Representation.* Boston, South End, 1992. https://www2.warwick.ac.uk/fac/arts/english/currentstudents/pg/masters/modules/femlit/bell_hooks.pdf.

Mulvey, Laura. "Visual Pleasure and Narrative Cinema." *In Film Theory and Criticism: Introductory Readings.* Edited by Leo Braudy and Marshall Cohen. New York: Oxford UP, 1999, 833–844. Available online at http://www.composingdigitalmedia.org/f15_mca/mca_reads/mulvey.pdf.

Pandika, Melissa. "Bra History: How a War Shortage Reshaped Modern Shapewear." *NPR,* August 5, 2014. http://www.npr.org/2014/08/05/337860700/bra-history-how-a-war-shortage-reshaped-modern-shapewear.

Singer, Maya. "Hear Us Roar: Finding Feminism in Fashion." *Vogue,* September 5, 2014. http://www.vogue.com/article/finding-feminism-in-fashion.

Summers, Chelsea G. "The Politics of Pockets." *Racked,* September 19, 2016. http://www.racked.com/2016/9/19/12865560/politics-of-pockets-suffragettes-women.

Thorpe, J. R. "The History of the Tampon—Because They Haven't Always Been for Periods." *Bustle,* November 19, 2015. https://www.bustle.com/articles/124929-the-history-of-the-tampon-because-they-havent-always-been-for-periods.

INDEX

ABOUT THE AUTHOR

Trained as an evolutionary biologist, Amber J. Keyser cares deeply about the intersection of art and science. Her recent nonfiction titles include *Tying the Knot: A World History of Marriage*, *Sneaker Century: A History of Athletic Shoes*, and *The V-word*, an acclaimed anthology of personal essays by women about first-time sexual experiences. Her young adult novels include *Pointe, Claw*, an explosive novel about two girls claiming the territory of their own bodies, and *The Way Back from Broken*, a heart-wrenching novel of loss and survival, which was a finalist for the Oregon Book Award. She is also the coauthor with Kiersi Burkhart of the middle grade series *Quartz Creek Ranch*. Learn more about her at www.amberjkeyser.com.

PHOTO ACKNOWLEDGMENTS

The images in this book are used with the permission of: iStock.com/jammydesign, p. 1; Ron Galella, Ltd./WireImage/agency/Getty Images, p. 5; Courtesy Youtube, p. 6; Sonia Halliday Photo Library/Alamy Stock Photo, p. 9; China Photos/Getty Images, p. 11; REUTERS/Michaela Rehle, p. 13; Rühe/ullstein bild/Getty Images, p. 16; FineArt/Alamy Stock Photo, p. 20; ACTIVE MUSEUM/Alamy Stock Photo, p. 21; © Laura Westlund/Independent Picture Service, p. 22; Nationalmuseum/Wikimedia Commons (CC BY-SA 4.0), p. 23; Pictorial Press Ltd/Alamy Stock Photo, p. 24; Chronicle/Alamy Stock Photo, p. 27; ART Collection/Alamy Stock Photo, p. 28; Danita Delimont/Alamy Stock Photo, p. 29; ClassicStock/Alamy Stock Photo, p. 31; Pictorial Press Ltd/Alamy Stock Photo, p. 32; INTERFOTO/Alamy Stock Photo, p. 33; Everett Collection Historical/Alamy Stock Photo, p. 35; © Todd Strand/Independent Picture Service, p. 37; © Manet, Edouard (1832-83)/Hamburger Kunsthalle, Hamburg, Germany/Bridgeman Images, p. 38; The Granger Collection, New York, p. 40; Wikimedia Commons (Public Domain), p. 43; Popperfoto/Getty Images, p. 44; Fine Art Images/Heritage Image/Getty Images, p. 45; Chronicle/Alamy Stock Photo, p. 47; Alfred Eisenstaedt/Pix Inc./The LIFE Picture Collection/Getty Images, p. 49; Photo 12/Alamy Stock Photo, p. 51; Shaw Family Archive/Alamy Stock Photo, p. 52; Image courtesy of The Advertising Archives, pp. 54, 61; Bettmann/Getty Images, pp. 55, 56; JON LEVY/AFP/Getty Images, p. 59; Courtesy Julian Rios Cantu, p. 63; REUTERS/Babu, p. 64; Via https://wearpact.com, p. 67; Frank Micelotta/ImageDirect/Getty Images, p. 69; Sebastien Micke/Paris Match/Getty Images, p. 71; Robert Landau/Alamy Stock Photo, p. 73; Gideon Barnett/Studio LHOOQ, p. 74; Image via Dear Kate p. 77; © Independent Picture Service, p. 80; © DAVID J SWIFT/The New York Times/Redux, p. 81; Raymond Hall/GC Images/Getty Images, p. 82; Via https://www.neonmoon.co, p. 83; Leila Navidi/Minneapolis Star Tribune/TNS/Newscom, p. 85.

Front cover: Horst P. Horst/Conde Nast/Getty Image; iStock.com/Tabitazn (letters).